Accent Reduction Tutorial

Katrina Dahl

Edited by
Christopher Erle &
Jacqueline Tobin

Copyright © 2018 Katrina Dahl
First Published Huge Jam, London 2018
All rights reserved.
ISBN: 978-1911249269

Cover Images by rawpixel, Serkan Turk, Victoria Heath, katemangostar, Taylor Grote. Designed by Huge Jam.

CONTENTS

	Introduction	1
1	Evaluation Vowels	3
2	Evaluation Consonants	23
3	Evaluation Results/Overview	52
4	Consonant Fundamentals	56
5	Vowel Fundamentals	80
6	Intonation	109

INTRODUCTION

"Hello, my name is Katrina Dahl. I created this book as a tool to be used by instructors and students. The users of this book can use parts or the book as a whole. In consideration of different teaching and learning styles, I tried to present the same material in different ways. I have learned that when learning to reduce accents, practice is very important, the student must understand and perfect phonemes in isolation, and the learner must continually perfect all the sounds of one of the paragraphs that incorporate all the phonemes. I hope you have as much fun using this book as much as I had writing it. Enjoy."

CORRECTION TOOL BOX

Below is a list of suggestions of things you can do if a student needs to correct their sounds.

1. Find the closest sound they have and work from there. For example, if they are able to say /k/ but not /g/, then perfect the /k/ sound then add the voice part to produce /g/.
2. Sometimes the student needs to improve their phonetic awareness for the sound. So if the say "bat" instead of "bad", make them aware and say, " Is it bat or bad (with a slight emphasis on bad to give them a little more time to hear the difference)." Also have two cards. One with "t" and the other "d". Once they say a sound, ask them to point to the sound they think they said. Sometimes you may be surprised that they first need to work on identifying the sound before they can correctly produce it.
3. Take the closest sound they know, tell them to stop their tongue there and tell them where to move the tongue to make the correct sound. For example, if they "sh" instead of "s". Tell them to make the "sh" sound, hold their tongue where it is, then move their tongue more forward and flatten the tongue a bit more.
4. When students can inconsistently produce the sound, tell them to produce *it* wrong then right then wrong then right. Repeating after you. Say "bat" then "bad" then "bat" then "bad". This helps them get a better "feel" for producing the sound correctly.
5. Use a linking sound. For example, if the student can produce the sound in the initial position but not in the final position, use a first word that ends with the difficult sound and the next word that starts with the difficult sound. For example, "bad dog." The difficult sound can also be linked with a sound that they can do before their problem sound.
6. Explain the sound anatomically on a diagram.
7. Explain how to produce the sound using your mouth or a model mouth.

THE EVALUATION - VOWELS

The simplest accent reduction begins with vowels, because vowels are easier for most clients to produce, as they are unvoiced and demand less activity from the articulators. Each vowel sound will be tested in the initial, final, and then medial position. The reason for placing the medial position words last is that it is the most difficult position to properly pronounce a target sound in. Each sound has a chart, which is divided into initial, final, and medial sections. Each section has a target word, a sentence, and a blank space. Have the client say each target word. Then have the client say the sentence provided, which uses the target word. Finally, have the client make a sentence that uses the target word. At the bottom of each chart is a section for notes. Since this is only an evaluation, do not correct or guide the client's speech. If he/she does not know how to pronounce a word and asks you to tell them, ask how he/she *thinks* it should be pronounced. The evaluation is meant to assess their strengths and weaknesses as they are.

A.1 – introducing the client to the IPA sound system at the word and sentence levels

Most people know nothing about, or have never heard of, the International Phonetic Alphabet (IPA). Thusly, they are not aware of the full range of sounds made by speakers of other languages besides their own. The purpose of the initial part of the evaluation is to expose the client to sounds in the IPA system that he/she has either never heard or never truly practiced. Additionally, some clients may be familiar with sounds, either having heard or having made them, in one position of speech (for example, the initial position) but not in other positions of speech. It is particularly difficult for people with foreign accents to produce unfamiliar sounds in the medial position, where the articulators have the least time to get into position for the sound.

Things to Consider During the Evaluation

- Types of errors or disfluency (i.e.. tongue thrust for /s/, deletions, substitutions)
- Percentage of errors in each position
- Stimulability and at what positions
- Are there helper sounds that facilitate correct articulation of target sound?
- Notice intonation and vocal loudness (i.e.. do statements sound like questions?)
- What's the client's overall tone (i.e.. low, overly-contracted?
- What is the client's resting mouth posture?
- Is there a lip/facial droop affecting speech?
- Does the head move independently from the tongue…in both the native and English languages?
- Are longer words more difficult than shorter words?
- Note their breath support for speech
- Are certain sounds more difficult in certain speech environments (i.e. is a sound more difficult when said in a consonant cluster, or if a front sound is preceded by a back sound)?

/i/

Initial

eat	I went to eat a sandwich this afternoon.	This space is for the client's sentence using the same sound

Final

all_ey_	I parked my car in the alley behind the store.	

Medial

t_ea_ch	Someday, I want to teach math.	

This space is for your notes on the client's production of each IPA sound.

_____
_____
_____
_____
_____
_____
_____

/I/

Initial

| inside | There is a grand piano inside this house. | |

Final

Some sounds do not occur in either the initial, final, medial, or some combination of the three. In American English, /I/ does not occur in the final position of any words.

Medial

| lift | He likes to lift weights. | |

/eɪ/

Initial

<u>a</u>ble	Is she able to get it herself?	

Final

p<u>ay</u>	I have to pay the rent in one week.	

Medial

occ<u>a</u>sion	What occasion are we celebrating today?	

/ɛ/

Initial

| enter | Please, enter the building quietly. | |

Final

| sound does not occur in the final position. |

Medial

| letter | Did you read the letter I wrote for you? | |

/æ/

Initial

| apple | Today I picked an apple off of a tree. | |

Final

| sound does not occur in the final position |

Medial

| basket | He put the flowers in her basket. | |

/ɑ/

Initial

| offer | They offered me some cherries, but I declined. | |

Final

| p<u>aw</u> | The dog licked his paw quietly. | |

Medial

| c<u>au</u>tioun | You should approach the road with caution. | |

Accemt Reduction Tutorial

/ɔ/

Initial

| oak | Meet me by the oak tree this afternoon. | |

Final

| fl<u>ow</u> | We sat and admired the flow of the river. | |

Medial

| l<u>o</u>cal | Are you a tourist or a local? | |

/oʊ/

Initial

| owed | I owed her twenty dollars last week. | |

Final

| show | He would love to show you his collection of books. | |

Medial

| sewing | She will join us after her sewing is done. | |

/ʊ/

Initial

sound does not occur in the initial position

⬇

Final

sound does not occur in the final position

⬇

Medial

b<u>oo</u>k	Have you finished writing your book?	

⬇

/u/

Initial

<u>oo</u>zes	Watch as the volcano oozes lava.	

Final

d<u>o</u>	No one knows how to do that.	

Medial

ass<u>u</u>med	He assumed the role of leader in his father's absence.	

/ə/

Initial

about	It's about time we arrived.	

Final

comma	This sentence should have a comma.	

Medial

oven	Did I turn off the oven before I left the house?	

/ʌ/

Initial

| other | You should use the other spoon instead. | |

Final

| sound does not occur in the final position |

Medial

| mother | Mother has certainly taught us well. | |

/ɜr/

Initial

| urge | I urge you to reconsider. | |

Final

| philosopher | I am a thinker, but I am no philosopher. | |

Medial

| girls | All the girls have black hair. | |

/aɪ/

Initial

| aisle | Please keep the aisle clear for the flight attendant. | |

Final

| apply | Apply glue to the paper and wait for it to dry. | |

Medial

| mighty | The lion made a mighty roar. | |

/aʊ/

Initial

| <u>ou</u>tside | We are having a barbeque outside. | |

Final

| h<u>ow</u> | How did they do that? | |

Medial

| p<u>ow</u>erful | Allison is a powerful woman. | |

/ɔI/

Initial

| oysters | I love to eat oysters. | |

Final

| annoy | The puppy was trying to annoy me. | |

Medial

| royalty | We were treated like royalty. | |

A.2 – Applying the IPA sound system at conversational level

Now that the client has pronounced each of the words given and used them at the sentence level of speech, it is time for them to use those words at the conversational level. Producing sounds at the conversational level can be much more difficult, and people often feel overconfident when it is not as difficult to produce the sounds correctly at the word or sentence level. This is because the client is afforded time and consideration in saying the word on its own or in a short sentence. Conversational exercises, however, demand that the client has a mastery of the words and does not hesitate before saying them. Any hesitations on his/her part (at the word, sentence, or conversational levels) should be noted. When it is no longer a challenge to correctly pronounce words at the rapid pace of conversation, then a mastery of the American English accent has been achieved.

Below are several paragraphs which, in total, use all of the words from the word and sentence level evaluation. Each line in the paragraphs has a blank line underneath it. Have the client read each paragraph aloud and note underneath the line he/she is reading what mistakes or changes have been made and whether or not those mistakes are consistent, inconsistent, or only occurring at the conversational level of speech.

Evaluative Paragraph 1

I prefer to eat outside, although most people eat inside. The one thing I enjoy more than oysters is fresh air, and having both makes me feel like royalty. It helps to lift my spirits so that I might be able to teach local students in math and letters. Every day I bring a basket of food for lunch. I always keep an apple with me. I enter the courtyard and sit under the oak tree to enjoy my meal. On special occasions, or when my oven doesn't work, I pay the market for other meats and cheeses. I urge my students to eat lunch outside with me as often as I can. The girls do this more than the boys.

Evaluative Paragraph 2

My mother may not be a philosopher, but she is a mighty woman with a powerful voice. She speaks up if something annoys her. She would always apply herself well in her work, and I have always assumed that she got her way. She is also very helpful. Once we found a dog in an alley that was hurt. It had glass in its paw. She approached it with caution, but still wanted to show that she meant to help. We wrapped the dog's paw so that the blood would not ooze anymore, and we took it home with us! I was very proud of her that day.

Evaluative Paragraph 3

I would like to tell you how I came to love books so much. I used to take the bus to my job, and that offered me the opportunity to do whatever I wanted on the way there. At first, I took up sewing, but I did not keep up with it at all. I had to think of something else to do that would make time flow more swiftly. A friend said that I should read more, but I didn't know much about books. In fact, I could barely use a comma! I never liked to read as a child, but I trusted her advice and tried it anyway. With nothing else to do on the bus, I would sit in the aisle and try to imagine the characters in the stories I read. I began to love imagining those things. I now know that I owed reading a real chance, because I have grown to love it.

THE EVALUATION - CONSONANTS

Consonants are often more difficult to pronounce correctly, both because they employ a wider range of articulator (tongue, lips, teeth, jaw, throat) placement and because some are pronounced without a vibration. This vibration is known as voicing. The phenomenon of voicing does not apply to all vowels, as all vowels are unvoiced sounds. A voiced consonant, such as /b/, will utilize vibration in order to sound correctly, while an unvoiced consonant, such as /t/, will be pronounced without vibration of the vocal chords. Some consonants are produced with identical placement of the teeth, tongue, lips, and jaw but differ in whether or not they are voiced. This creates a reciprocal relationship between consonants, /b/ and /p/ being an example of this. /b/ is the voiced version of /p/, or one could say that /p/ is the unvoiced version of /b/. When explaining this difference to a client, place his/her hand over the throat during the pronunciation of a consonant. The client should be able to feel his/her throat vibrating upon producing a voiced sound and should feel no vibration when producing an unvoiced sound. Do this with reciprocal consonants to enforce the similarity in pronunciation technique and the significance of voicing.

A.1 – Introducing the client to the IPA sound system at word and sentence levels

Most people know nothing about, or have never heard of, the International

Phonetic Alphabet (IPA). Thusly, they are not aware of the full range of sounds made by speakers of other languages besides their own. The purpose of the initial part of the evaluation is to expose the client to sounds in the IPA system that he/she has either never heard or never truly practiced. Additionally, some clients may be familiar with sounds, either having heard or having made them, in one position of speech (for example, the initial position) but not in other positions of speech. It is particularly difficult for people with foreign accents to produce unfamiliar sounds in the medial position, where the articulators have the least time to get into position for the sound.

/p/

Initial

| pack | I must pack for our vacation. | |

Final

| ship | Have you ever been on a ship? | |

Medial

| appetite | His son has quite an appetite this evening. | |

/b/

Initial

| boast | My mother taught me not to boast. | |

Final

| ca<u>b</u> | Please call a cab for me. | |

Medial

| a<u>b</u>le | Are you able to work tomorrow? | |

/t/

Initial

| tired | The class was very tired yesterday. | |

Final

| date | I am going on a date tonight. | |

Medial

| data | We will collect data for the experiment. | |

/d/

Initial

<u>d</u>istance	Alice is more of a distance runner.	

Final

sa<u>d</u>	It was a sad day for everybody.	

Medial

a<u>d</u>orable	That puppy is adorable.	

/k/

Initial

| kettle | I will get a kettle on for our tea. | |

Final

| back | They came back so soon after they left. | |

Medial

| accent | This accent adjustment program will help me. | |

/g/

Initial

| good | Lisa is a good person. | |

Final

| fog | I can't see through all of this fog. | |

Medial

| figure | We should be able to figure this out. | |

/tʃ/

Initial

| chin | He shaves everything apart from his chin. | |

Final

| catch | Robert does not catch as well as he throws. | |

Medial

| attachment | Their attachment is sweet. | |

/w/

Initial

| waiter | The food is awful, but the waiter is hilarious. | |

Final

| Some sounds do not occur in either the initial, final, medial, or some combination of the three. In American English, /w/ does not occur in the final position of any words. |

Medial

| highway | I took the highway to get to California. | |

/dʒ/

Initial

| juggle | He would like to learn to juggle. | |

Final

| stage | The stage is set and the players are ready. | |

Medial

| adjust | We will have to adjust our approach. | |

/f/

Initial

| fast | Vanessa is a very fast driver. | |

Final

| laugh | Bobby knows how to make me laugh. | |

Medial

| offer | Adrian's offer was hard to refuse. | |

/v/

Initial

| violet | Violet is a beautiful color. | |

Final

| save | A lifeguard must save people in danger. | |

Medial

| favorite | What is your favorite color? | |

/θ/

Initial

| thinking | I'm thinking about moving to Seattle. | |

Final

| ba<u>th</u> | This dog needs a bath. | |

Medial

| li<u>th</u>ograph | I have been studying a lithograph in school. | |

/ð/

Initial

| this | I would like my room to look like this one. | |

Final

| ba<u>the</u> | They want to bathe in the lake. | |

Medial

| mo<u>th</u>er | His mother is such a nice woman. | |

/s/

Initial

| silly | Adam made a silly face at me. | |

Final

| glass | A greenhouse has glass walls. | |

Medial

| fossil | There was a fossil in his backyard. | |

/z/

Initial

| zest | I like to use lemon zest in my cooking. | |

⬇

Final

| shoes | Mandy can't find her shoes. | |

⬇

Medial

| losing | She is losing this race. | |

⬇

/ʃ/

Initial

| shock | It was a shock to see them together. | |

Final

| cash | I gave him cash for the movie. | |

Medial

| fishing | Let's go fishing tomorrow morning. | |

#

Initial

Some sounds do not occur in either the initial, final, medial, or some combination of the three. In American English, /ʒ/ does not occur in the initial position of any words.

Final

| mirage | I saw a mirage in the desert. | |

Medial

| meaure | Always measure carefully when cooking. | |

/r/

Initial

| royal | That girl is of royal blood. | |

Final

| car | Do you own a fast car? | |

Medial

| irrelevant | The lawyer's questions were irrelevant. | |

/h/

Initial

| hands | He likes to work with his hands. | |

Final

| Some sounds do not occur in either the initial, final, medial, or some combination of the three. In American English, /h/ does not occur in the final position of any words. |

Medial

| be<u>h</u>avior | Be on your best behavior this eveing. | |

/l/

Initial

| language | I will practice speaking the English language. | |

Final

| banal | His banal speech left me very bored. | |

Medial

| benevolent | Her spirit was very benevolent. | |

/m/

Initial

| manage | Alex wants to manage a bar someday. | |

Final

| fla_m_e | Don't stand too close to the flame. | |

Medial

| da_m_age | The damage to the house was minimal. | |

/n/

Initial

| natural | A fear of heights is natural. | |

Final

| done | I am done working on that project. | |

Medial

| money | How much money do you have left? | |

/ŋ/

Initial

Some sounds do not occur in either the initial, final, medial, or some combination of the three. In American English, /ŋ/ does not occur in the initial position of any words.

Final

asking	Be confident when asking questions.	

Medial

youngest	I am the youngest in my family.	

/j/

Initial

you	I like you very much.	

Final

Some sounds do not occur in either the initial, final, medial, or some combination of the three. In American English, /j/ does not occur in the final position of any words.

Medial

loyal	The knight was loyal to his king.	

A.2 – Applying the IPA sound system at conversational level

Now that the client has pronounced each of the words given and used them at the sentence level of speech, it is time for them to use those words at the conversational level. Producing sounds at the conversational level can be much more difficult, and people often feel overconfident when it is not as difficult to produce the sounds correctly at the word or sentence level. This is because the client is afforded time and consideration in saying the word on its own or in a short sentence. Conversational exercises, however, demand that the client has a mastery of the words and does not hesitate before saying them. Any hesitations on his/her part (at the word, sentence, or conversational levels) should be noted. When it is no longer a challenge to correctly pronounce words at the rapid pace of conversation, then a mastery of the American English accent has been achieved.

Below are several paragraphs which, in total, use all of the words from the word and sentence level evaluation. Each line in the paragraphs has a blank line underneath it. Have the client read each paragraph aloud and note underneath the line he/she is reading what mistakes or changes have been made and whether or not those mistakes are consistent, inconsistent, or only occurring at the conversational level of speech.

Evaluative Paragraph 4

Today I had to pack for our voyage on the ship. At first I could not even find my shoes. I didn't even know if I would be able to call a cab to pick me up from home. After all, I'm afraid to drive on the highway. The driver had a hard time understanding me because of my accent, but we managed to communicate. It was a long distance from my home to the bay where the ship was. I figured out how to show him where I was going by pointing at a map. He and I laughed at our struggle to find common language. When I got there, I told him that he was my favorite cab driver, and I offered to pay him extra. He refused to take anything. He told me that his mother would be angry if she knew that he charged me too much. Through the fog, I could see him waving goodbye to me through the glass windshield of his car.

Evaluative Paragraph 5

I wanted to learn to bake pastries, so I went to the store and bought some ingredients. Being in the store increased my appetite. Among other things, I bought flour, sugar, and lemons so I could use lemon zest in my sweets. I kept losing my grocery list while I was out shopping! It was a shock to me how expensive some ingredients were, and I hoped that I would have enough cash to pay for it all. I also purchased a measuring cup to help me follow the recipes I would be reading. Fortunately, I had enough money for everything. I wanted to learn to cook because I enjoy working with my hands, and the discipline of cooking would be good for my behavior. I did not want to depend on restaurants and waiters anymore. I am sure that a person like you can understand this feeling, since you are loyal to your kitchen. I intended to bake pastries worthy of royalty, and the fact that I had done this before was irrelevant to me. Despite my benevolent intentions, my first pastries were very banal, tasting plain and ordinary. I even burned my cupcakes, because the flame was too high in the oven. You could taste the damage on the bottoms and tops of the cakes! I suppose it is only natural that my first try was not so successful. They might have looked delicious, but that must have been a mirage.

Evaluative Paragraph 6

When our teacher was asking us about families, I said that I was the youngest in mine. She said, "What is your parentage?" I told her that my father was a German man who loved fishing and painting. My mother was a silly scientist who studied fossils and ancient data. My father always forgets important dates, but mother reminds him. Then I told them about the baths I took in the lake when my father was fishing. I would bathe with the fish for hours on end. My dad actually made a lithograph of me swimming in the sea once. He painted the waters with violet, saving blue for the fish. He stayed up all night to finish it fast. My adorable brother knows how to juggle and loves to be on stage. I tried to catch him on television last year balancing a chair on his chin, but I had just missed it. I feel that my attachment to my family is healthy. When I get back home tonight, we will all get the kettle on for our tea.

EVALUATION OVERVIEW

	Error/ comments for initial position	Error/comments for final position	Error/ comments for medial position	Error/comments at sentence level	Error/comments in paragraph or conversation
i					
ɪ					
eɪ					
ɛ					
æ					
ɑ					
ɔ					
oʊ					

Accemt Reduction Tutorial

	Error/ comments for initial position	Error/comments for final position	Error/ comments for medial position	Error/comments at sentence level	Error/comments in paragraph or conversation
ʊ					
ə					
ʌ					
ɝ					
aɪ					
aʊ					
ɔɪ					
p					
b					
t					
d					
k					
g					

	Error/ comments for initial position	Error/comments for final position	Error/ comments for medial position	Error/comments at sentence level	Error/comments in paragraph or conversation
tʃ					
dʒ					
f					
v					
θ					
ɣ					
s					
z					
ʃ					
ʒ					
h					
w					
j					

Accemt Reduction Tutorial

	Error/ comments for initial position	Error/comments for final position	Error/ comments for medial position	Error/comments at sentence level	Error/comments in paragraph or conversation
r					
l					
m					
n					
ɲ					

Additional Comments:

CONSONANT FUNDAMENTALS

Fundamentals

Voiceless and Voiced: Voiced consonants are those in which the larynx (or "Adam's apple" as it applies to men) vibrates as a result of the pronunciation of that sound.

IPA Sound System: Consonants

Symbol	Example	Possible Spellings
/p/	pigeon	p, pp
/b/	basket	b, bb, pb
/t/	brittle	t, tt, ed, ght, th
/d/	bread	d, dd
/k/	kettle	k, c, ck, cc, ch
/g/	gather	g, gg, gh, gue
/tʃ/	catch	ch, tch, ti, t, te, tu
/dʒ/	imagine	j, g, gg, dy, ge, dge, di
/f/	follow	f, ff, ph, gh
/v/	vessel	v, f, ph
/θ/	math	th
/ð/	this	th
/s/	satin	s, c, cc, sc, ps
/z/	zombie	z, zz, s, ss
/ʃ/	leash	sh, si, ce, ti, ci, s, ch
/ʒ/	siege	si, su, g, zi

Symbol	Example	Possible Spellings
/h/	hat	h, wh, j
/w/	wet	w, u, o, wh
/j/	yelling	y, i, u
/r/	terror	r, rr, wr, rh
/l/	illuminate	l, ll
/m/	master	m, mb, mn, mm
/n/	annotate	n, nn, kn, pn, gn
/ɲ/	fang	ng, ngue

Classification of Consonants

Plosives

Plosives are produced when air is completely blocked off by the articulators and is then released in a "puff", which can be heard/felt in the aftermath of pronouncing the "p" sound.

The following are the various plosives in the IPA:

Voiceless	Voiced
P	b
T	d
K	g

Plosive /p/: A voiceless sound produced by holding the two lips firmly together as breath is compressed inside the mouth. Then the lips suddenly part to release an explosion of breath through the mouth.

1. Practice: I should practice the steps for the big show.
2. Pallet: I need another pallet for these paints.
3. Camp: Tomorrow will be my first day at camp.

Co-articulation with /p/

	Initial	Final	Medial
/i/	peel	creep	leaping
/I/	pin	sip	dipper

	Initial	Final	Medial
/eɪ/	pain	cape	taping
/ɛ/	pen	step	leopard
/æ/	pan	lap	dapper
/ʌ/	pun	cup	supper
/u/	pool	loop	super
/ʊ/	push		
/ɔ/	pose	mope	interloper

Plosive /b/: A voiced sound produced by holding the two lips together firmly as the breath and voice is compressed inside the mouth. Then the lips suddenly part to release an explosion of the breath and voice through the mouth.

1. Bank – I must go to the bank this morning.
2. Pebble – Pebbles can be useful to jewelers.
3. Cab – I think I'll take a cab home.

Co-articulation with /b/

	Initial	Final	Medial
/i/	bean		feeble
/I/	bin	rib	sibling
/eɪ/	bate		fable
/ɛ/	best		pebble
/æ/	basket	cab	tabulate
/ʌ/	bun	cub	rubber
/u/	boost	lube	lubricant
/ʊ/	bull		
/ɔ/	bold	robe	sober

Plosive /t/: A voiceless sound produced by pressing the tongue's tip hard against the top back-ridge as the breath pressure of air builds up behind it. The tongue is quickly pulled away to release an explosion of breath.

1. Tasks – I gave Fred several tasks to complete.
2. Afternoon – In the late afternoon, he drinks tea.
3. Lift – It took a few men to lift the heavy sofa.

Co-articulation with /t/

	Initial	Final	Medial
/i/	tease	seat	liter
/I/	till	pit	babysitter
/eI/	tame	late	mating
/ɛ/	ten	net	wetter
/æ/	tassels	cat	matter
/ʌ/	tummy	rut	mutter
/u/	tools	root	scooter
/ʊ/	took	put	pusher
/ɔ/	total	coat	notation

Plosive /d/: A voiced sound produced like /t/ but with *voicing* added. Thusly, you should feel your larynx or "Adam's apple" vibrate with this sound.

1. Daylight – She only plays in broad daylight.
2. Daddy – Daddy said he would go to the store today.
3. Attitude – They always come to class with a positive attitude.

Co-articulation with /d/

	Initial	Final	Medial
/i/	deal	feed	leader
/I/	distance	lid	bidder
/eI/	date	made	raider
/ɛ/	den	fed	shredder
/æ/	dance	fad	padding
/ʌ/	dull	mud	muddy
/u/	duel	crude	prudish
/ʊ/		could	would've
/ɔ/	dome	load	exploding

Word Endings /t,d/

1. t/d are pronounced not as strong at ends of words, as they would be in initial positions ("doll", "day").

crept   moist   raft   just
world   sold   heard   gagged

2. If "ed" is preceded by a *voiceless* sound (p,t,k,f,th,θ,s,sh, tsh,h) it is pronounced as "t".

   lurched   crashed   attacked   trapped   iced
   missed   tipped   bashed   kicked   fished

3. If "ed" is preceded by a *voiced* sound, it is pronounced as "d".

   edged   razzed   loved   hoed   drowned   ribbed

4. When the verb ends in /d/ or /t/, the 'ed ending is pronounced as a separate syllable.

   ended   batted   seated   voted   patted   rotted

5. Pronounce –sts endings slowly & clearly as separate sounds.

Waists   posts   crusts   chests   masts   lists   wrists   trusts
Pastes   erupts   tastes   pastes   bests   dusts   tests   beasts

Plosive /k/: A voiceless sound produced by pressing the back of the tongue hard against soft palate as the air pressure of the breath builds up behind them. Quickly lower tongue to release explosion of the breath.

1. Back – Joe finally came back to see us.
2. Academic – Alex is a very successful academic.
3. Coffee – I always take my coffee with cream and sugar.

Co-articulation with /k/

	Initial	Final	Medial
/i/	keep	seek	peaking
/I/	kiss	sick	fickle
/el/	cave	lake	breaking
/ɛ/	kettle	neck	gekko
/æ/	candy	plaque	tackle

	Initial	Final	Medial
/ʌ/	cut	tuck	sucker
/u/	cool	duke	spooky
/ʊ/		book	rooky
/ɔ/	tone	note	floating

Plosive /g/: A voiced sound produced like /k/ but with voicing added. Thusly, you should feel your larynx or "Adam's apple" vibrate with this sound.

1. Gallon – I bought at gallon of milk at the market.
2. Tag – He forgot to remove the tag from his shirt.
3. Aggravating – The work was becoming very aggravating.

Co-articulation with /g/

	Initial	Final	Medial
/i/	geese		meagre
/I/	gift	rig	digging
/eI/	game		bagel
/ɛ/	guess	keg	beggar
/æ/	gander	sag	ragged
/ʌ/	gutter	plug	mugged
/u/	goose		
/ʊ/			booger
/ɔ/	golden		

Consonant Isolations in the Initial, Final, And Medial Positions

Consonants must be practiced in the same manner with which vowels are practiced, with each IPA consonant appearing in the initial, final, and then medial positions.

Phonetic Symbol	Typical Spellings	Initial Position	Final Position	Medial Position
[w]	w, wh	Winter		Owl
[m]	m, mm, mn	Major	Exam	Alabama
[p]	p, pp	Pencil	Stamp	Supper
[b]	b, bb	Best	Job	February
[f]	f, ff, ph	Fun	Stuff	Affiliate

Phonetic Symbol	Typical Spellings	Initial Position	Final Position	Medial Position
[v]	v, f	Valid	Stove	Evening
[]	th	Thirsty	Monolith	Stethoscope
[]	th	There		Neither
[n]	n, gn, kn, nn	Knitting	Dawn	Answer
[l]	l, ll	Laundry	Tall	Dollar
[t]	t, tt	Tongue	Matt	Fitness
[d]	d, dd	Dairy	Sad	Ladder
[j]	y, eu, u, li	Yack		Canyon
[s]	s, ss, c	Sister	Mass	Wrist
[z]	z, s, x	Zebra	Use	Laser
[]	sh, c, ch	Shore	Push	Ashes
[]	z, s, ge		Corsage	Measure
[]	c, ch, tu, tch	Chore	Match	Denture
[]	dg, g, d, j	Genetic	Damage	Illegitimate
[r]	r, w	Rapid	Error	Mermaid
[k]	k, ck, c, ch, q	Candle	Broke	Sticker
[g]	g, gg	Guilty	Wrong	Agree
[]	ng, n		Fang	Tangle
[h]	h	Handle		Inheritance

Minimal Pairs for Voiced vs. Voiceless Plosives

*Say the following sentences, initially using the first word in the parenthesis and then using the second word. Be sure to clearly recognize and pronounce the single phonemic difference between the two words.

1. I want a nice juicy (pear/bear).
2. I (punched/bunched) the bad to relieve tension.
3. How much was the (pill/bill)?
4. California has many (peaches/beaches).
5. Don't forget to (pack/back) your lunch.
6. I need a new (tie/dye) for my suit.
7. Park the boat near the (tock/dock).
8. I saw a (tuck/duck) in the pond.
9. They (tied/died) for first place.
10. Give him a good (tip/dip).
11. Let's play a game of (cards/guards).
12. It was a (cold/gold) day.
13. Which (crease/grease) do you recommend using?

14. She (came/game) home early.
15. I need my (coat/goat) to stay warm.

Nasals

There are three nasal consonants. All are voiced through the nose.

Nasal /m/: A sound produced by closing the lips (such as in the p/b consonants) and then lowering the soft palate and directing the voice through the nose. The sound produced is a hum.

1. Microscope – It was my turn to use the microscope.
2. Recommend – My teacher likes to recommend books to students.
3. Lamb – I had not eaten leg of lamb in a long time.

Co-articulation with /m/

	Initial	Final	Medial
/i/	meek	seem	seamstress
/I/	mill	brim	shimmer
/eI/	make	blame	famous
/ɛ/	mess	them	feminine
/æ/	mask	lamb	ramming
/ʌ/	much	from	newcomer
/u/	mood	loom	bloomer
/ʊ/			
/ɔ/	moan	gnome	chromosome

Nasal /n/: A sound produced by placing the tongue against the upper row of teeth and then directing the voice through the nose. The effect is very similar to that of /m/ and one can often be mistaken for the other.

1. Night – The night is so beautiful.
2. Sand – I love the feeling of sand between my toes.
3. Diminish – My flu has been diminished to a cold.

Co-articulation with /n/

	Initial	Final	Medial
/i/	neat	clean	meaning
/I/	nit	tin	litter

	Initial	Final	Medial
/eɪ/	nail	cane	raining
/ɛ/	nest	hen	rental
/æ/	Nancy	ran	landing
/ʌ/	nut	ton	blunder
/u/	noose	moon	crooning
/ʊ/	nook		
/ɔ/	nose	prone	tonal

Nasal "ng" /ŋ/: A sound produced by placing the tongue against the back of the palate/roof of the mouth, as if producing a /g/. Then direct the voice through the nose. The result is the /n/ sound with a barely noticeable /g/ at the end of it.

1. Linger – Why does she always linger around him?
2. Sing – I love to sing!
3. Bringing – Are you bringing the pie to my party?

Co-articulation with /ŋ/

	Initial	Final	Medial
/i/		ring	mingle
/I/			
/eɪ/			
/ɛ/			
/æ/		sang	anger
/ʌ/		lung	dungaree
/u/			
/ʊ/			
/ɔ/			

Glides

/r/, /l/, /j/, /w/ are all glides. They are called glides because they have very little initial "attack" in their pronunciation, whereas a plosive consonant is very strong initially. This allows these consonants to glide into vowels and other consonants smoothly.

/r/: A sound produced by placing the tongue in the center of the mouth and rolling the tip of the tongue inward. Remember to keep the lips neutral.

1. Rake – I need to purchase a new rake for my lawn.
2. Rates – Those insurance rates are too high.
3. Care – Does he care if we leave without him?

Co-articulation with /r/

	Initial	Final	Medial
/i/	reach	peer	leering
/I/	rich		terrify
/eI/	rain	lair	Lorraine
/ɛ/	rest		serotonin
/æ/	ran	avatar	sarcastic
/ʌ/	rust		chorus
/u/	rude	endure	purest
/ʊ/	rooky		duration
/ɔ/	Rome		

/l/: A sound produced by flattening the tongue against the roof of the mouth.

1. Lower – May I take the plane lower?
2. Allow – I will not allow you to do that.
3. Pillow – I need to fluff your pillow before you sleep.

Co-articulation with /l/

	Initial	Final	Medial
/i/	leech	peal	sealant
/I/	litter	fill	silicone
/eI/	late	pale	ailment
/ɛ/	letter	shell	pelican
/æ/	landing	pal	California
/ʌ/	luster	dull	blunder
/u/	loose	fool	aloof
/ʊ/	look		
/ɔ/	loan	soul	rolling

/w/: A sound produced by placing the tongue in the upper area of the back region of the mouth and rounding the lips. The tongue will always move when pronouncing this sound in the direction of the vowel it will be attached to.

1. What – What are you looking at?
2. Awhile – It's been awhile since we went out.
3. West – Head west if you want to get to Seattle.

Co-articulation with /w/

	Initial	Final	Medial
/i/	wheel		leeway
/I/	wit		`Edwin
/eI/	waste		bewail
/ɛ/	weather		Midwest
/æ/	wagon		beeswax
/ʌ/	wonder		no one
/u/	woo		
/ʊ/	wood		
/ɔ/	woke		awoken

/j/: A sound produced by placing the tongue against the roof of the mouth and then immediately upon pronunciation sliding the tongue into the vowel that /j/ is gilding into.

1. Jail – I hope I never go to jail.
2. Jimmy – Jimmy really is a nice guy.
3. Pager – Dose anybody use a pager anymore?

Co-articulation with /j/

	Initial	Final	Medial
/i/	jeep		
/I/	Jim	bridge	diligent
/eI/	James	page	staging
/ɛ/	Jeff	ledge	indulgence
/æ/	janitor	badge	
/ʌ/	just	fudge	nudging
/u/	juice		bejeweled
/ʊ/			
/ɔ/	joke		cogent

Fricatives

There are 4 pairs of fricative consonants and a voiceless "h" sound. Each pair is made of a voiced and a voiceless consonant.

Voiced	Voiceless
F	v
th- ð	TH- θ
S	Z
sh- ʃ	zh- Z
	h

/f/: A voiceless sound produced with the top teeth on bottom lip with breath forced through.

1. feel – I feel safe in this stuffy place
2. raffle – Fred raffled fresh fries and stuffing last Friday.
3. grief – The calf suffered a lot of grief.

Co-articulation with /f/

	Initial	Final	Medial
/i/	feel	chief	stuffy
/I/	finish	plaintiff	benefit
/eI/	fate	safe	deface
/ɛ/	fetch	clef	confess
/æ/	fan	calf	laughter
/ʌ/	fun	stuff	buffer
/u/	food	aloof	goofy
/ʊ/	foot	hoof	thoughtful
/ɔ/	phone	loaf	townsfolk

/v/: A voiced sound produced with the top teeth on bottom lip with breath and voice forced through.

1. veal – Valerie cooked veal and vegetables for dinner.
2. voice – Vicky has a lively voice.

3. view – The view of the valley is very nice.
4. live – Live life to its fullest.
5. save – He saved a life that day.

Co-articulation with /v/

	Initial	Final	Medial
/i/	vehicle	leave	diva
/ɪ/	Victor	live	giving
/eɪ/	veil	brave	raven
/ɛ/	vest		leverage
/æ/	van		ravenous
/ʌ/		dove	shoving
/u/		move	grooves
/ʊ/			
/ɔ/	vote	stove	nova

/s/: A voiceless sound produced by curling the sides of the tongue and pushing the breath through the narrow middle groove between the tongue.

1. seal – I saw a seal in the sea.
2. slim – See the slim, slick, and slender saplings.
3. seep – The sauce seeped through all the pots.
4. less – She chose the less fattening oil.
5. messy – His room is always so messy.

Co-articulation with /s/

	Initial	Final	Medial
/i/	seek	peace	thesis
/ɪ/	simple	bliss	mister
/eɪ/	save	brace	chasing
/ɛ/	set	mess	vessel
/æ/	sand	brass	castle
/ʌ/	subtle	bus	muscle
/u/	soon	moose	loosen
/ʊ/	soot		
/ɔ/	sold	dose	

/z/: Is produced like /s/ with the addition of **voicing.**

1. zebra – He was a fan of the zebra.
2. always – Zack always brings his zipper.
3. pads – Add pads to those roads.
4. muzzle – Her dog was forced to wear a muzzle.
5. cousin – My zesty cousin lives next door.

Co-articulation with /z/

	Initial	Final	Medial
/i/	zebra	cheese	easy
/I/	zipper	his	business
/eI/		maze	Daisy
/ɛ/	zest	says	Leslie
/æ/	Xander	Spaz	
/ʌ/		buzz	cousin
/u/	zoom	ooze	choosing
/ʊ/			
/ɔ/	zone	hose	nosey

S/Z Rules

1. "es" at the end of a word is pronounces as the extra syllable "iz" if the verb ends in "s, z, ch, dg"

| gloss-es | dish-es | ooz-es | pass-es | mouse's | wish-es | judg-es | pag-es | hatch-es |
| smash-es | mass-es | botch-es | walrus-es | scratch-es | match-es | siz-es | catch-es | quiz-es |

2. If a final "s" is preceded by a *voiceless* consonant, it is pronounced as an "s."
(p-t-k-f-th-s-tsh-h)

      bats   thief's   laps   kicks   huffs   hits
   spoofs   decks   sifts   moths   scout's   Judith's

3. If a final "s" is preceded by a *voiced* sound, it is pronounced as a "z"

lids	sings	sees	runs	fills	dogs
times	loves	shows	jails	roars	fads
kid's	mom's	Bob's	teacher's	girls'	city's

S/Z Distinctions in Words

peace-peas	fleece-fleas	cease-seas hiss-his
ass-as	loose-lose	juice-Jews purse-purrs
curse-curs	hearse-hers	bus-buzz pace-pays
lace-lays	race-rays	trace-trays grace-graze
lice-lies	gross-grows	base-bays mace-maize

S/Z Distinctions in Sentences

1. It pays to walks at a fast pace.
2. The bays each had a naval base.
3. Those Jews loved juice.
4. There were fleas on the fleece of geese.
5. The rays of the sun were bothering the runners in the race.

/th/: A voiceless sound produced by placing the tongue tip between the teeth. Push breath out through tongue and teeth.

1. theme – Think of three thrilling themes.
2. faith – Ethel and Martha have a lot of faith.
3. youthful – It's healthy to think of youthful thoughts.
4. south – They will fly south for the winter.
5. thousand – It took a thousand men to build the temple.

Co-articulation with /th/

	Initial	Final	Medial
/i/	theme	teeth	
/I/	thin	monolith	mythical
/eI/			
/ɛ/	theft	breath	breathless
/æ/	thank	wrath	mathematics
/ʌ/	thump		
/u/		booth	throughout

	Initial	Final	Medial
/ʊ/			
/ɔ/		growth	

/TH/: A voiced sound produced by placing the tongue tip between the teeth. Push breath and voice through tongue and teeth.

1. breathe – Breathe this as you bathe.
2. other – why bother to see the other brother?
3. that – That sheathe is theirs.
4. then – I was younger back then.
5. leather – She refuses to wear leather.

Co-articulation with /TH/

	Initial	Final	Medial
/i/	these	seethe	breathing
/I/	this		wither
/eI/	they	scathe	bathing suit
/ɛ/	then		leather
/æ/	that		gathering
/ʌ/	thus		mother
/u/		smooth	soothing
/ʊ/			
/ɔ/	those	clothing	loathe

TH/th Rules

1. Almost all initial "th" sounds are pronounced as /θ/ - "th" with some exceptions.
   Exceptions (pronounced "TH")
   the, this, that, these, those, than their, them then, they, though

thank	thaw	theft	theme	thigh	thing
think	third	thirst	thorn	thought	thump

2. The voiceless "th" at the end of words almost always is pronounced as voiced "TH" *when it changes to plurals.* For example, path – paths, the "th" is voiceless in path but is pronounced as voiced "TH" in paths.

bathes   mouths   clothes   paths   teethes   wreathes

3. Final "th" is usually the voiceless "th".
   Exceptions: *bathe, breathe, clothe, smooth, soothe, teethe, wreathe*

aftermath   eightieth   fiftieth   fortieth   ironsmith
monolith   overgrowth   sixtieth   tablecloth   thirtieth
twentieth   underneath

4. "TH" in the middle position in words is pronounced as the voiced "TH" when *followed by "er"*.

another   feather   southerner   gathering   lather   leather
mother   sunbather   together   weatherman   weatherproof   father

5. Final "TH" followed by "e" is generally pronounced as voiced "TH".

bathe   clothe   soothe   teethe   wreathe   writhe

/sh/: A voiceless sound produced similarly to /s/ but lips more rounded and extended.

1. shells – She sells sea shells on the seashore.
2. shine – Shelly shines at the show.
3. glacier – The shine glacier hit my shin.
4. crash – She lashed out after the crash.
5. shack – Shy Shelly lives in a shack.

Co-articulation with /sh/

	Initial	Final	Medial
/i/	sheets	leash	facetious
/I/	ship	dish	delicious
/eI/	shave		satiate
/ɛ/	shelter	mesh	pressure
/æ/	shack	cash	dashing
/ʌ/	shudder	lush	brushes
/u/	shoes		
/ʊ/	shook	push	pushing
/ɔ/	showman		social

/zh/: A sound produced similarly to /sh/ but with more voicing.

1. mirage – The mirage was a pleasurable illusion.
2. decision – Make the usual, casual decision.
3. closure – I need closure to this unusual vision.
4. persuasion – She needs persuasion and precision before making the decision.
5. vision – Your vision of treasure was a mirage.

Co-articulation with /zh/

	Initial	Final	Medial
/i/		siege	seizure
/I/			fissure
/eI/		beige	
/ɛ/			pleasure
/æ/			
/ʌ/			
/u/		street luge	
/ʊ/			
/ɔ/			

/h/: A voiceless sound produced like a voiceless vowel with forced air out. /h/ does not have a voiced counterpart.

1. hold – Harry happily holds his hat.
2. hardly – Hurricanes hardly happen in New Hampshire.
3. hiding – Harold was hiding under the unheated house.

Co-articulation with /h/

	Initial	Final	Medial
/i/	heel		behind
/I/	history		uphill
/eI/	haste		behave
/ɛ/	heather		bellhop
/æ/	hassle		forehand
/ʌ/	hustle		manhunt
/u/	whom		yoo-hoo
/ʊ/	hood		fishhook
/ɔ/	haughty		overhaul

Afficates

There are two afficates, the voiceless /tsh/ and the voiced /dzh/.

/tsh/: A voiceless sound produced similarly to /sh/ but with /t/ exploding into /sh/ to make the /tsh/ sound.

1. cheap – Charles bought cheap chips and cherries.
2. catch – I watched the chair fall into the ditch.
3. coach – The coach pitched the ball to each player.
4. rich – The rich man punched the chair by accident.
5. cheer – You may choose to either chant or cheer.

Co-articulation with /tsh/

	Initial	Final	Medial
/i/	cheese	breach	teacher
/I/	chiseled	stitch	pitcher
/eI/	chase		Rachel
/ɛ/	chest	stretch	Duchess
/æ/	chastity	match	Apache
/ʌ/	chump	touch	crutches
/u/	choose	pooch	suture
/ʊ/			
/ɔ/	Chaucer	watch	Rochester

/dzh/: A voiceless sound produced similarly to /zh/ but with /d/ exploding into /zh/ to make the /dzh/ sound.

1. large – The large hedgehog hit the ridge.
2. jam – Jack had jam and juice.
3. judge – The judge put the underage juvenile in jail.
4. joke – Jay and John tell great jokes.
5. jewels – Jason bought Jade jewels.

Co-articulation with /tsh/

	Initial	Final	Medial
/i/	jeep		congeal
/I/	gypsy	bridge	eligible
/eI/	James	cage	arranging

	Initial	Final	Medial
/ɛ/	gentle	pledge	regiment
/æ/	jackal	badge	exaggerate
/ʌ/	just	fudge	adjustable
/u/	juice	huge	adjudicate
/ʊ/	jury		
/ɔ/	jaunty	dodge	lodge

Consonant Minimal Pairs

/p/	/b/
pill	bill
prim	brim
paul	ball
rip	rib
maple	mabel
ample	amble
pumpkin	bumpkin
simple	symbol
staple	stable
apportion	abortion
pearly	burly
oppressed	abreast
pup	pub
pus	bus
push	bush
tripe	tribe
prude	brewed
swapping	swabbing

/ʒ/	/ʃ/
Confucian	confusion
aleutian	allusion
asher	azure
dilution	delusion

/ð/	/θ/
thigh	thy
sheath	sheathe
mouth	mouths

/ð/	/θ/
teeth	teethe
wreath	wreathe

/s/	/z/
advice	advise
abuse	abuse
buses	buzzes
bruce	bruise
ceasing	seizing
close	close
hearse	hers
grace	graze
fussy	fuzzy
once	ones
niece	knees
sip	zip
use	use
victorious	Victoria's
excuse	excuse

/f/	/v/
fest	vest
life	live
raffle	ravel
few	view
half	halve
belief	believe
defied	divide
elfish	elvish
fail	veil
fast	vast
define	divine
thief	thieves
strife	strive
wafer	waiver
file	vile

/l/	/r/
alive	arrive
pleasant	present

/l/	/r/
walling	warring
splint	sprint
plop	prop
plodding	prodding
pliers	priors
lusty	rusty
plank	prank
mallow	marrow
mandolin	Mandarin
lower	rower
long	wrong
mislead	misread
liver	river
ling	ring
limb	rim
leaf	reef
glean	green
fairly	fairy
collection	correction

/t/	/d/
ant	and
ten	den
tech	deck
tears	dears
writer	rider
written	ridden
clout	cloud
colt	cold
kit	kid
watt	wad
matter	madder
bitten	bidden
bite	bide
abort	aboard
betting	bedding
freight	frayed
fort	ford
fate	fade
sweeten	Sweden

/t/	/d/
sunburned	sunburnt
tab	tat
pleat	plead
plate	plaid

/m/	/n/
marrow	narrow
beam	bean
boom	boon
famed	feigned
trams	trans
warm	warn
tumor	tuner
someday	Sunday
sperm	spurn
smuggling	snuggling
mode	node
mine	nine
mashing	gnashing
mere	near
gum	gun
gnome	known
dimmer	dinner
combs	cones
clam	clan

Consonants at the Conversational/Narrative Level

Back in college, I had a major exam in the winter. I was studying in Boston, but I was born in Alabama. It was February at the time of the exam, and I woke up realizing that I hadn't studied! I ran to my car, past a foreboding owl, only to find that I did not have any pencils; they were all in my house. I was so frustrated, because I had to run back into my house to retrieve a pencil. My sister was very helpful. She must have pitied me! Once I got into the car, I bit my tongue, and my teeth felt more like fangs than teeth. It was so painful that I had to wait several minutes before I could drive to class. Eventually, I pushed myself to arrive, with my tongue damaged and a feeling of sheer disappointment in myself. I don't handle the feeling of failure well. I decided that I shouldn't be so negative. After all, I had not failed yet! I could have strolled into class, given the test my best try, and had confidence in myself. Unfortunately, I did not get the chance to prove myself. I woke up in a frantic, dashing seizure for nothing. It was Saturday. The test would not be for two more days.

VOWEL FUNDAMENTALS

*The vowel(s) in a word carry the most information in the identification of a word. Therefore, it is critical that you have perfect pronunciation of the vowel sounds in order to be a clear and effective speaker.

- Vowel sounds are made with very little obstruction in the vocal tract
- It is the movement of the articulators (lips, tongue, jaw) and the degree of tension in the cavity that distinguish one vowel from another.
- Unlike consonants, vowels are not easy to hear, feel, or see and, thusly, must be practiced much more.
- All vowels are voiced sounds. That is, they require the vocal cords to vibrate in order to pronounce them.
- A consistent issue is that American English is not phonetic so words and phrases are not always pronounced as they are spelled. There are usually many possible spellings for one vowel. For example, the word "people" seems as though it would be pronounced /pi o pl/ or /pE o pl/. It is with these irregularly pronounced words that the implementation of IPA is especially important.
- IPA vowel sound pronunciation must be practiced at the word, sentence, and conversational levels.

IPA Sound System: Vowels

Symbol	Example	Possible Spellings
/i/	_e_asy	ea, ee, e, ie, ei, I, eo, oe, uay, ae, y
/I/	_i_nput	i, e, u, ee, u, y, ei
/eI/ or /e/ • These two IPA symbols represent the same sound in the IPA system. However, the first is a dipthong and the second is a monothong. For the purposes of this text, the sound will be taught as both monothong and dipthong so as to encourage the maximum amount of versatility.	d_a_te	a, e, ai, ay, ei, ey, ea, ue, ee, au, a_e, et
/ɛ/	d_e_nt	e, ue, ea, a, ie, ai
/æ/	_A_dam	a, ai
/ɑ/	t_o_ppings	a, ea, o, aw, ow, au, oa
/ɔ/	f_ou_ght	o, a, ou, oa, aw, ow
/oʊ/ or /o/	s_ew_ing	o, oa, ow, oe, ou, eau, oo, au, o_e
/ʊ/	l_oo_k	o, oo, u, ou
/u/	s_u_perstitious	u, ue, ew, o, ou, oe, iu, wo, u_e
/ə/	ov_e_n	a, u, oi, u, ei, ai, e, I, oo, o, e
/ʌ/	_o_thers	Ia, ah, oe, u
/ər/	lov_er_	ur, er, or, ar, ure, yr, oar
/ɜr/	f_ur_	ur, er, ir, ear, or, our
/ɑI/	th_igh_	i, y, uy, ei, eye, ui, i_e
/aʊ/	f_ow_l	ou, ow, au
/ɔI/	empl_oy_	oi, oy

Classifying Vowels

*Classifications are implemented in the description of vowels - referred to in *Sound Features*.

Front, Central, Back

Vowels are grouped as front, central, or back vowels depending on where the highest part of the tongue is during production. (See vowel placement chart.)

		Mouth/Jaw	Tongue Placement	Tongue Tension	Lips
Front Vowels	/i/	high	forward	tense	retracted
	/I/	high	forward	lax	slightly retracted
	/eI/ /ɛ/	high-mid mid	forward forward	mid lax	mid-retracted neutral
	/æ/	low	forward	lax	neutral
Central Vowels	/ə/ /ər/ /ʌ/	neutral neutral neutral	center center center	neutral neutral neutral	neutral neutral neutral
Back Vowels	/u/	high	back	tense	rounded
	/ʊ/	high	back	lax	rounded
	/oʊ/	mid-high	back	mid	increasingly rounded
	/ɔ/	mid	back	lax	slightly rounded
	/ɑ/	low	back	lax	neutral

High, Mid, Low

High, mid, and low vowels describes the height of the tongue/jaw during a particular sound.

Lax/Tense

The amount of tension in the tongue during vowels contributes to their clarity.

Lip Position

Notice that the lips seem more rounded, retracted, or neutral for certain vowels.

- Rounded: lips form "o" shape
- Retracted: lips are pulled back into a smile and show teeth at various degrees.
- Neutral: lips are neither positioned forward nor backward

Vowel Length

Although one should take time to produce all vowels, some vowels are slightly longer than others.

Tongue Movement in Relationship to the IPA Vowel Grid

*Vowels are generally more difficult to pronounce because they demand more peculiar positions for the lips and tongue.

Have the client practice pronouncing the following IPA vowel sounds in words and then to entire sentences (as seen on the next pages).

FRONT VOWELS

Front vowels are those vocalized with the tongue positioned in the front of the mouth.

/i/

Sound features: high, lips slightly retracted, tense, long
Spelling options: ea, ei, e, ie, ee, i_e, ey, e_e

Words

teacher	seat	believe	she	grieve	receive
preach	decent	alley	peas	keep	team
evening	see	decent	easy	heat	steep

Sentences

1. I see pizza on my ceiling.
2. I love to eat ice cream, pizza, and peas.
3. I want to peacefully sleep this evening.
4. It's easy to succeed with teamwork.
5. She is a decent teacher.
6. I've been meaning to tell you to keep up the good work.
7. He leaned against the walls of the alley.
8. I have to teach this evening.
9. I can see a basket of peaches.
10. I will keep the award I am about to receive.

/I/

Sound features: mid-high, lips slightly retracted, lax, short
Spelling options: I, e, y, u, y

Words

sister	litter	lips	bitter	lyric	system	enlist	eyelid
ripple	crisp	history	ribbon	kiss	print	inhibit	relationship
mistake	limit						

Sentences

1. My <u>thin</u> sister is also pretty and simple.
2. I <u>finished</u> the dishes and fed the fish.
3. I <u>printed</u> a big picture of a fish.
4. The <u>little</u> ribbon has an interesting print.
5. The <u>list</u> of history dates seems limitless.
6. <u>Mister</u> Smith made a mistake.
7. Later on, we <u>kissed</u> on the lips.
8. I <u>missed</u> history class three times.
9. <u>This</u> package is tied with a ribbon.
10. The drink was too <u>bitter</u> for my limits.

/eI/

Sound features: mid, lips retracted, tense, long
Spelling options: a, ia, ei, a_e, ey

Words

page	faith	play	tray	railroad	eight	state
essay	lazy	occasion		crayon	rave	pace
rake	tape	late		gave	crave	

Sentences

1. I <u>gave</u> the label to Stacy.
2. My <u>neighborhood</u> has railroads and many pathways.
3. I <u>baked</u> the eighty cakes on the plate.
4. That <u>stranger</u> is insane.
5. I <u>gave</u> Paige a lacey brace.
6. For my <u>sake</u>, please get a new rake.
7. She has no more <u>tape</u> for you to take.
8. On this <u>occasion</u>, I am feeling lazy.
9. The <u>eight</u> of us went out of state.
10. I <u>stayed</u> up late finishing my essay.

/ɛ/

Sound features: mid, lips slightly retracted, lax, short

Spelling Options: e, ea, ue

Words

let	fell	prevent	head	when	better
bent	weapon	quest	pretzel	dead	reject
dead	tennis	tenth	set	lesson	empty

Sentences

1. Shelly <u>sent</u> my bet to Stella.
2. The <u>shell</u> fell in the cellar.
3. Ben played <u>ten</u> <u>sets</u> of <u>tennis</u>.
4. Jen <u>sent</u> the health trend projects to Ben.
5. I sent <u>ten</u> red pens to Jen.
6. Life is full of <u>lessons</u> when you ask questions.
7. My <u>pencil</u> case is empty.
8. I'll <u>let</u> you rent my room.
9. The <u>weapon</u> fell out of his vest.
10. I <u>meant</u> to prevent that accident.

/æ/

Sound Features: low, lips slightly retracted, lax, short
Spelling Options: a, au

Words

anger	rapid	sad	lack	past	bath
valley	demand	tank	lamp	fact	basket
brat	cat	lasting	fast	past	laugh

Sentences

1. The <u>sad</u> cat ran rapidly across the tracks.
2. Sandy <u>demanded</u> a basket of fabulous stamps.
3. Sam relaxed after he captured the nasty <u>rat</u>.
4. I <u>laughed</u> and clapped after the magic show.
5. Stan's <u>dad</u> accidentally yanked the elastic off his napkin.
6. She <u>ran</u> towards the orange cat.

7. <u>Janis</u> wants a bed that will last.
8. <u>After</u> the game, he took a bath.
9. I need a <u>stand</u> for my lamp.
10. The market will <u>expand</u> very fast.

CENTRAL VOWELS

Central vowels are those vocalized with the tongue in the center of the mouth.

/ɜr/

Sound features: middle of tongue arched, neutral lips
Spelling options: ur, er, ir, ear, or, our

Words

surrender	learn	earnest	merge	faster	reverberate
Earth	fern	confer	plural	earner	learner
journey	curse	precursor	pearls	perks	circumstance

Sentences

1. She was wearing <u>pearls</u> that evening.
2. Some lessons are harder to <u>learn</u> than others.
3. <u>Plural</u> <u>words</u> can be difficult to remember.
4. Of the two, he is the primary <u>earner</u>.
5. From the beginning, his <u>journey</u> was <u>cursed</u>.
6. We will <u>confer</u> and make a decision.
7. The company <u>merger</u> was a change for everybody.
8. We all listened as the drums <u>reverberated</u>.
9. The <u>faster</u> I work, the <u>faster</u> I'll finish.
10. <u>Turn</u> right at the stop sign.

/ə/

Sound features: middle of tounge arched and slightly raised, neutral lips
Spelling options: a, u, oi, u, ei, ai, e, I, oo, o, e

Words

sudden	about	syrup	occur	open	affect
pigeon	cupboard	arrive	oven	announce	

Sentences

1. <u>Suddenly</u> I felt as if I was being taken away.
2. What was that book <u>about</u>?
3. He was happy before the accident <u>occurred</u>.
4. Did you find it in the <u>oven</u>?
5. Their words did not <u>affect</u> me.

/ʌ/

Sound features: low, neutral lips, lax, short
Spelling options: u, o, oo, ou

Words

Luck	front	stubborn	rug	lunch
Some	sullen	supper	flood	stuck
Up	put	pulse	double	color

Sentences

1. My <u>cousin</u> is coming up here in a couple of months.
2. I <u>love</u> making tons of money.
3. The <u>government</u> is cutting the budget this month.
4. I <u>won</u> a large sum of money.
5. My <u>cousin</u> sometimes makes a big fuss.
6. I'm <u>stuck</u> at work until lunchtime.
7. She stood in <u>front</u> of the stubborn horse.
8. <u>Up</u> the street from me are some great shops.
9. I <u>cut</u> my hand while preparing supper.
10. Your <u>rug</u> is the same color as my car.

/ɑ/

Sound Features: low, neutral lips, lax, short
Spelling Options: o, a
found in a Boston or Boston-like accent

Words

hot	pocket	rocks	rotten	solid	proper
want	jog	rob	somber	top	wander
honest	doll	shop	cobweb	clock	prompt

Sentences

1. I put the hot rocks in my pocket.
2. My honest college friend wandered all day long.
3. I found a great fossil rock at the sports shop.
4. The rock-shaped clocks have cobwebs on them.
5. I want to jog with the fox.
6. I bought the best dolls in the shop.
7. I always lock the door to my loft.
8. He's going to wash his clothes in hot water.
9. A man was robbed at the top of the building.
10. The proper way to shake hands is firm and solid.

BACK VOWELS

Back vowels are those vocalized with the tongue in the back of the mouth.

/ɔ/

Sound features: low, lips rounded, lax, short
Spelling options: au, aw, o, ou, a, augh

Words

pauper	clause	haughty	soft	cough	caution
loft	pauper	taught	fault	haunt	faucet
yawn	frost	thaw	thought	saw	author

Sentences

1. I <u>taught</u> the pauper how to yawn.
2. I <u>thought</u> the author told haunted stories.
3. The <u>gaudy</u> woman yawned a lot.
4. Have <u>caution</u> when you gawk and yawn too much.
5. I <u>saw</u> a hawk taunt another hawk.
6. I <u>thought</u> I should walk to school today.
7. Be <u>cautious</u> when using the faucet.
8. We must <u>thaw</u> the frost on the engine.
9. I was <u>caught</u> yawning at the party.
10. That year in <u>Australia</u> taught me many things.

/O/

Sound features: low, lips rounded, tense, long
Spelling options: o, oa, ou, ow, o_e, ew

Words

old	coke	coat	broke	close	bony
most	road	remote	blow	roast	soul
roll	boulder	zodiac	coast	go	foam

Sentences

1. This old colt is bold and cold.
2. Most of the foam on the road has blown away.
3. The boulder broke the robot.
4. The old coal broke down the barn door.
5. My goal is to win a new boat at the rowing coast contest.
6. Joseph has fragile bones.
7. his T.V. has no remote control.
8. I am sorry that I broke the toaster.
9. Go prepare the foam for the bubble bath.
10. Rock and Roll is my favorite kind music, but soul is good also.

/U/

Sound features: mid-high, lips slightly rounded, lax, short
Spelling options: u, o, oo, ou

Words

crook	took	bully	butcher	cookie	foot
push	pudding	book	look	should	cook
good	input	wool	bullet	cushion	ambush

Sentences

1. The butcher pushed the wood under the table.
2. I should have cooked pudding instead.
3. Push the pulley into the brook.
4. A woman could have been the crook.
5. I took my wool hood to the cleaners.
6. That pudding took a long time to make.
7. You could use bullet points in your outline.
8. I pushed Alice to give her input.
9. Those cushions are made of wool.
10. I like to look at photography books.

/u/

Sound features: high, lips rounded, tense, long
Spelling options: e, u, oo, ui ou, ew, oe, u_e

Words

rumor	fuse	suit	drew	moose	cruel
June	movie	noon	ruin	school	shoe
true	bruise	soup	clue	lose	new

Sentences

1. I threw the new shoe away.
2. I don't have a clue about what you put in the soup.
3. I soon will buy a new suit.
4. The movies in June start at noon.
5. I approve of the new room that will be added to the school.

6. It is true that I have many shoes.
7. I must use this movie ticket.
8. We lit the firework fuse and enjoyed the view.
9. The spilt coffee ruined my new suit.
10. I usually lose my glasses.

Vowel Isolations in the Initial, Final and Medial Positions

IPA VOWEL EXERCISES

Phonetic symbol	Initial position	Final position	Medial position
/i/	easy	remedy	feel
/I/	input	------------	spin
/eI/	aviation	today	date
/ɛ/	edible	------------	mentor
/æ/	after	------------	last
/ɜr/	earn	faster	curse
/ʌ/	affect	mantra	fumble
/u/	ooze	moose	true
/ʊ/	------------	------------	good
/oʊ/	over	throw	hold
/ɑ/	awesome	saw	clock
/aI/	ion	tie	flight
/aʊ/	outer	growl	mouth
/ɔI/	ointment	deploy	disappoint

In order to reduce the totality of an accent, the client must practice the pronunciation of IPA vowels in the initial, final, and medial positions. Exercise pronunciation of vowels in the initial and final positions and then medial, as it is the most difficult (see chart above for words with IPA vowels in all three positions).

Vowel Length

A vowel within a stressed syllable is held longer before a voiced consonant than before a voiceless consonant. For example, "cab" (vowel before voiced consonant) is said longer than "cap" (vowel before an unvoiced consonant).

Vowel Length Exercise:
Word Pairs (Voiced And Unvoiced Consonants)

say the following word pairs with particular consideration for syllable stress and voiced/unvoiced consonant position in relation to vowel length

B	P
cab	cap
cub	cup
ribbed	ripped
symbol	simple
dabble	dapple
gab	gap
lab	lap
slab	slap
swab	swap
abe	ape
Mable	maple
mob	mop
nab	nap
tab	tap
pub	pup
rib	rip
robe	rope
tribe	tripe
stable	staple
nib	nip

G	K
bug	buck
league	leak
chug	chuck
snigger	snicker
pig	pick

G	K
brig	brick
lagging	lacking
dog	dock
bag	back
haggle	hackle
rag	rack
Doug/dug	duck
jog	jock
hog	hock
frog	frock
flag	flack
hag	hack

D	T
add	at
bide	bite
bowed	boat
bud	but
cad	cat
cod	cot
fade	fate
Fred	fret
lewd	loot
fried	fright
grade	great
need	neat
laid	late
loud	lout
owed	oat
raid	rate
ride	right
road	wrote
wide	white
tried	trite

DZ	TS
badge	batch
besiege	beseech
edge	etch
large	larch

DZ	TS
Madge	match
range	ranch
ridge	rich
purge	perch
marge	march
surge	search

V	F
dove	duff
five	fife
knives	knife
strive	strife
wave	waif
believe	belief
prove	proof
grieve	grief
leave	leaf
live	life
raffle	ravel
rival	rifle
save	safe
serve	surf
of	off
have	half
sheave	sheaf
shovel	shuffle
calve	calf

Z	S
braize	brace
bruise	Bruce
clothes	close
grows	gross
doze	dose
dues	deuce
fleas	fleece
flaws	floss
joys	Joyce
knees	niece
laws	loss

news	noose
peas	piece
raze	race
spies	spice
saws	sauce

Hold vowels LONGER when followed by a VOICED sound
Pronounce vowels SHORTER as WORDS get LONGER

←-------LONG-----------	----------MEDIUM----------	---------SHORT----------→
Sin	Singe	Cinch
Mar	Marge	March
Row	Robe	Rope
Low	Lobe	Lope
Ma	Mob	Mop
Try	Tribe	Tripe
Lay	Leg	Lake
Bay	Beg	Bake
Lee	League	Leak
Say	Save	Safe
Sir	Serve	Surf
Lie	Live	Life
Lee	Leave	Leaf
Say	Save	Safe
Sir	Serve	Surf
She	Sheaves	Sheaf
Rye	Rise	Rice
Die	Dies	Dice
Ray	Raze	Race
Gray	Graze	Grace
Pea	Peas	Peace
Eye	Eyes	Ice
You	Use	Use
Pry	Prize	Price
Saw	Saws	Sauce
Lie	Lies	Lice

Bay	Bade	Bait
No	Node	Note
Play	Played	Plate
Fee	Feed	Feet
Way	Wade	Weight
Fry	Fried	Fright
Lie	Lied	Light
Go	Goad	Goat
Row	Road	Wrote
Rue	Rude	Root
He	Heed	Heat
Sigh	Side	Sight
Try	Tried	Trite
Tow	Toad	Tote
Brew	Brewed	Brute
Why	Wide	white

Vowel Minimal Pairs

-Minimal pairs are any two words differing by only one phonetic component (i.e. "found" and "phoned")

-Exercises with minimal pairs are intended to develop more precise pronunciation and eliminate difficulties with co-articulation.

MINIMAL PAIRS EXERCISE

ɔI	O
soiled	sold
poised	posed
coin	cone
join	Joan
toy	tow
oiled	old
loin	loan
hoist	host
coils	coals
toil	toll

ɔI	o
Joy	Joe
boil	bowl

aU	o
sow	sew
found	phoned
route	wrote
now	no
towels	tolls
town	tone
bound	boned
housed	hosed
bowels	bowls
clown	clone
drown	drone
arouse	arose
bough	bow

æ	ʌ
stabbed	stubbed
rag	rug
back	buck
ham	hum
ran	run
hang	hung
rash	rush
match	much
tack	tuck

a	o
bald	bold
ox	oats
rod	road
balls	bowls
hall	hole
gall	goal
cot	coat
stalled	stole
john	joan
knot	note
tod	toad
walk	woke

I	ɛ
trick	trek
lift	left
six	sex
bill	bell
disk	desk
bit	bet
picked	pecked
din	den
pin	pen
bitter	better

aU	aI
mouse	mice
found	find
flowers	flyers
route	write
bowel	bile

aU	aI
ground	grind
bound	bind
foul	file
brown	brine
town	tine
round	rind
rouse	rise
mound	mind

aI	I
wise	whiz
tyke	tick
hide	hid
liked	licked
slide	slid
time	tim
right	writ
sight	sit
stripes	strips
sigh	sin
mice	miss
pine	pin
lied	lid

aI	e
vine	vein/vain
wife	waif
line	lane
lie	lay
bike	bake
guise	gaze
wines	wanes

aI	e
pile	pale
file	fail
lice	lace
lied	laid
light	late
fried	frayed
might	mate
time	tame
tile	tail
rind	rained

ɔI	aI
soy	sigh
boy	buy
toy	tie
foil	file
toil	tile
lawyer	liar
oil	aisle
point	pint
boil	bile
loin	line
voices	vices

ʊ	u
stood	stewed
pulled	pooled
soot	suit
look	Luke
hood	who'd
guck	gook
looks	Luke's

ɑ	ʊ
shock	shook
lock	look
hockey	hooky
box	books
rock	rook
cock	cook
hocked	hooked
knock	nook
crock	crook
botch	butch
wad	wood

ʌ	ɑ
buddy	body
mums	mom's
lulled	lolled
come	calm
cup	cop
stumped	stomped
gut	got
duck	dock
pup	pop
nut	not

æ	ɑ
cap	cop
rat	rot
sack	sock
black	block
stack	stock
mapped	mopped
racket	rocket

æ	a
rack	rock
bland	blonde

ɛ	æ
begged	bagged
pet	pat
bend	band
men	man
leg	lag
ken	can
met	mat
send	sand
lettuce	lattice
fellow	fallow

I	e
pill	pail
still	stale
trill	trail
pins	pains
bill	bail
bid	bade
mill	mail/male
mitt	mate
stick	stake/steak
fill	fail

e	ɛ
laid	led/lead
sprayed	spread
tasted	tested
pain	pen
braids	breads
rake	wreck
jail	gel
lace	less
raced	rest
based	best
trade	tread
mace	mess
bail/bale	bell

i	e
meal	mail
kneel	nail
deal	dale
weed	wade
teal	tail/tale
week/weak	wake
sleet	slate
heal	hail/hale
feeling	failing

I	i
seat	sit
teens	tins
sleek	slick
sleep	slip
weeps	whips
neat	knit
seed/cede	sid
each	itch

I	i
peal/peel	pill
deal	dill
reach	rich
beads	bids

i	ɛ
meat/meet	met
keen	ken
wheat	wet
seal	sell/cell
dean	den
cheek	check
peeked	pecked
reach	wretch
steam	stem
feel	fell
read	red
feed	fed

/I/	/æ/
pill	pal
simple	sample
rift	raft
lifter	laughter
gills	gals
blister	blaster
Jim	jam
kitsch	catch
zip	zap

/ɑ/	/ɔ/
cot	caught
tot	taught
not	naught

/oʊ/	/ɔ/
boat	bought
loan	lawn
phone	fawn
low	law
sew	saw

CONVERSATIONAL LEVEL EXERCISES

The following narrative makes use of the words in the previous vowel exercises. Read the narrative out loud and pay particular attention to the length and positions of vowels in the words. Remember, these are words that have already been exercised at the word and sentence level. This exercise just places them in a cumulative paragraph.

Today I lost my wallet. It's true! When I was getting ready to leave my apartment this morning, it was nowhere to be found. I searched my entire home- my kitchen, bedroom, living room, spare bedroom, and closets. Where on Earth could it have been? A wallet is such a precious item to lose, and I feel so flawed for losing it. Most of the time, it has been throw over my pants from the night before. I never have to fumble through my clothes to find it. It was such bad luck that it felt like there was a curse on me. I may have to cancel my date tonight if I can't find it. The last time this happened was over a year ago! It's a good thing that I'm so calm about it and not growling at every person I see. It would be easy to lose my head over this. I am definitely disappointed, but at least I know where I last saw it. It was next to my tie. Perhaps I'll try to look there.

Now try reading another paragraph out loud.

Jessica has a very interesting family. Her father, Aaron, is a painter who teaches art at a university in Vermont. He likes to paint with watercolors, and Salvador Dali is his favorite artist of all time. He enjoys telling her stories of his escapades all over the world. He has been to Europe many times in his life. Secondly, Jessica's mother, Olivia, used to be a ballet dancer. She originally met Aaron when she was an artist's model at his university. Olivia then went to Russia to perform Swan Lake, a famous ballet production, and returned to the United States to be with Aaron. Her parents have a remarkable love story. She is the younger one of two children. Her brother's name is Daniel. Daniel is currently in college. He is studying astronomy and is more of a scientist than an artist, unlike his parents. Jessica is in her third year of high school and looks forward to graduating and becoming a photographer. Her family is proud of her, and she is just as proud of her family.

Chapter Summary

- All vowels are voiced sounds.
- Vowels are classified by the configurations of articulators used to pronounce them as front, back, or central vowels.
- Clients must practice use of all IPA vowels in the initial, final, and medial positions of words.
- Client must practice the application of different vowel lengths and stresses in different conversational scenarios to ensure fluidity of speech.

Minimal pairs are words which differ by only one phonetic element and can be used to isolate pronunciation difficulties or to assist a client who cannot easily recognize a given IPA sound.

INTONATION

Intonation of American English

Correct sentence structure and accurate pronunciation are both very important elements in clear, uninhibited speech; however, there is more to one says than the words he/she uses. In person-to-person (as opposed to over the telephone or through email) conversation, there are verbal and nonverbal communications working together to convey an idea. A relaxed posture from a communicator may give the recipient the idea that the subject matter is frivolous, convincing him/her to relax as well. Inversely, an upright posture and taught facial expression from the same communicator may give the recipient the impression that the subject matter is very significant, or possibly even offensive. Much of the implementation of body language in person-to-person conversation is not particularly conscious. Instead, it often manifests in the form of a set of recurring mannerisms (or gestures), which may be unique, in their combination and regularity, to that particular person. Simply put, every person has "their way" of expressing themselves. These conscious and subconscious signals help the communicator to guide the recipient, emphasizing a particular mood, statement, word, or even a specific syllable (this often occurs in the emphasis of a prefix or suffix) and are often referred to as body language.

Another way in which the communicator may precisely express him/herself is with the use of **intonation**. Intonation is a varying combination of pitch, stress, duration (the length of a word or syllable), and speech rate (which is equivocal to duration, but applied to phrases). These four components of intonation work similarly to the aforementioned use of body language in that they guide the recipient's decoding and interpreting of the communicator's message. For example, an increased pitch in the predicate of a sentence places greater emphasis on what the subject is doing, as opposed to the subject itself. Increasing the duration of an adjective like *pretty* or *nice* will give the impression that it is the main point of the statement, or of the whole conversation. Proper and judiciously used intonation gives the communicator control of how they are listened to (i.e. a moving political speech), but careless or inconsistent intonation can just as easily confuse the listener(s), making them vulnerable to communication error (such as thinking that a friend is bothered by something when he/she is not).

Listen to the Accent Reduction Accompaniment Disc to hear examples of how intonation can direct conversation.

Pitch

While more distinctive and precisely tonal in its musical context, **pitch** still characterizes conversational speech and is affected by both vocal quality and the stress element of intonation (meaning that the emotive or emphatic state of the communicator will affect the pitch of key words). Every language (as well as regional dialect) has its own method of manipulating pitch in different speech situations (such as casual, business formal, family formal, etc.).

Levels of Pitch

American English consists of 4 degrees of pitch, typically called **pitch levels**, which ascend or descend depending on the emphasis, dialect, and style of the communicator.

Fig. 1

As seen in Figure 1, phonemic elements of non-regional American speech occur within these 4 levels of speech. Casual, relaxed speech usually occupies levels 2 and 3, as well as the spaces in between those levels (later discussed in *Glides*). Levels 1 and 4 are used for special emphasis, though they lie on diametrically opposite ends of the pitch spectrum. Level 1 is often used in the beginning and ending of statements, encapsulating the expression. It is also utilized in expression low emotive states or exhaustion. Level 4 is used to place high, unmistakable emphasis on words or syllables.

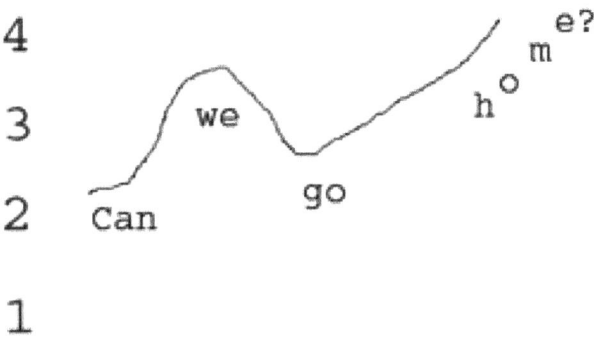

Fig. 2

Demonstrated in Figure 3, pitch can affect both syllables at the word level of speech and entire words at the sentence and conversational levels of speech.

Steps and Glides

Pitch variations in speech occur in the form of either **steps** or **glides**. When entire syllables in a word are said within different pitch levels, those syllables are vocalized in steps. The displacement in pitch levels between two syllables in step-vocalization is called a **step change** (see figure 3).

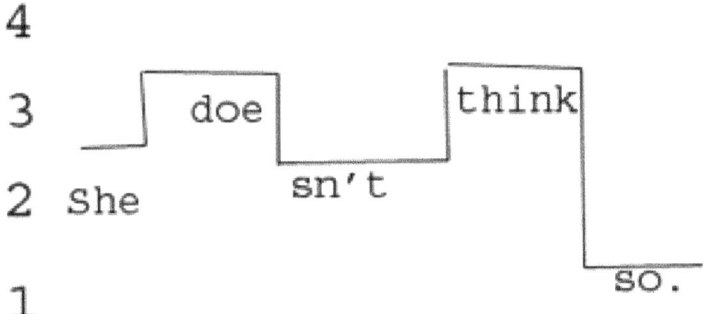

Fig. 3

The Accent Reduction Accompaniment Disc has examples of step changes in speech.

A glide occurs when the pitch in a syllable changes, rising or falling between the four levels of pitch and creating transitions between the syllables in a word. Since the rising or falling pitch in one syllable is carried on by the next, the syllables (especially the vowel elements) will slide into one another comfortably and elongate in doing so. Glides create smoother, less fragmented pronunciations of words (as seen in Figure 4).

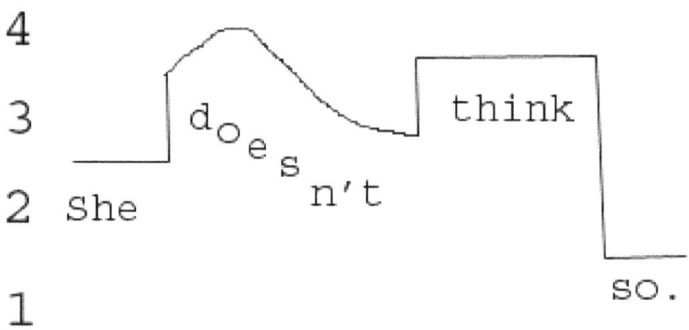

Fig. 4

Refer to the Accent Reduction Accompaniment Disc to hear how glides can affect speech.

There are 3 types of glides, each of which has a corresponding symbol in pitch-diagramed speech; these are rising, falling, and slightly rising pitch.

SLIGHTLY RISING   RISING   FALLING

Fig. 5

Listen to the Accent Reduction Accompaniment Disc to hear the 3 types of glides in speech

Stress

Conversational speech is full of variation and color. Without this spectrum of delivery, the communicator would sound dull, monotonous, and robotic. The proper use of **stress**, much like proper pitch (as previously mentioned), is one of the four constituents of natural, well-rounded speech. Stress, contrary to the connotations of the word, can do more than increase the pressure of a topic in conversation. It can also be used in relaxed dialogues, as it highlights key words and phrases in a sentence. The tactful use of stress in communication is also a very significant element in the equation of humor, emphasizing the punch line of a joke or the focal point of an anecdote.

Stress may manifest in one of three forms (which can be implemented simultaneously):

VOLUME – using a significantly louder voice to distinguish a particular prefix, suffix, or a particular word in a sentence.

PITCH – raising the pitch of a vowel or an entire word. The more drastic the increase in pitch, the greater the sense of urgency in the word is.

LENGTH – elongating a vowel or a word in a sentence or phrase in order to accentuate it.

Stress is most commonly described as occurring in one of three levels. There are actually five or six levels of stress, depending on each speech pathologist's system, but for the purpose of this book and the majority of speech pathology, only three levels are necessary.

— **PRIMARY**   __ **SECONDARY**   • **WEAK**

As seen above, the levels of stress in speech are (in descending order) **primary, secondary,** and **weak**. More important syllables in words (at the word level) and more important words (at the sentence level) receive higher levels of stress than supporting words and syllables. Because the first syllable in a word (especially a key word/focal point) is the most important, it is usually pronounced with *primary* stress, while the following syllables are pronounced with secondary or weak stress (the last syllable is typically the least stressed). Much of this emphasis and prioritization in communication is understood intuitively, but this intuition is often clouded when learning a second language, as the speaker's familiarity with his/her first language influences the flow of his/her speech in a new language. The result is unnatural sounding speech that does not accurately convey the feelings and intentions of the communicator. An understanding of stress will also benefit recipients of speech, as they will be able to discern undertones of humor, sarcasm, and seriousness with greater speed and confidence.

Intonation at Word Level

There are eight fundamental patterns of intonation in the formal American English dialect, each of which applies at both the word and sentence/phrase levels. Despite having so few patterns of intonation with which to say anything, the American English dialect mixes them so frequently that a wide range of conversational and formal tones can be easily and intuitively manipulated. The words used in the following exercises may appear in more than one intonation pattern. The words used in each pattern are meant to exemplify that pattern, but it is not necessarily the only way that those words may be expressed.

For all the Pattern Exercises that follow, please listen also to the audio tracks that accompany them.

PATTERN 1

The first pattern is simply a falling **pitch curve** on a single syllable. It is most commonly placed at the end of statements that convey information with emotional neutrality.

Intonation Pattern 1, Exercise 1

Say the following words with a falling pitch curve. Then say the words with a slightly rising pitch curve (as though you were asking a question or making an implication), and listen to the difference.

lace	sweat	press	dwarves	cans	farm
bells	quack	charm	through	can't	smell
codes	Gwen	ruff	birth	count	lamps
yes	host	sell	spring	snack	stamp
what	passed	silk	length	dimes	film
twice	stand	shores	month	smoke	bloom

PATTERN 2

The second pattern of intonation is similar to the first. The difference is that there are two syllables. The first syllable receives weak stress (which cannot occur simultaneously with a pitchcurve), and the second syllable receives the falling pitch curve found in Pattern 1.

Intonation Pattern 2, Exercise 1

Say the following words with weak stress on the first syllable and a falling pitch curve on the second syllable.

domain	expect	suggest	decide	duty	freehand
boyfriend	nifty	ladies	labor	color	witchcraft
filmstrip	journal	resolve	unsolved	million	value
angels	extinct	nasal	sizzle	throughout	compose
magnet	dental	frenzy	Spencer	suspense	appoint
agent	ribbon	boxing	paddle	savings	Wednesday

PATTERN 3

—
.

The third pattern applies primary stress to the first syllable in a two-syllable word and weak stress to the second syllable. Unlike Patterns 1 and 2, there are no pitch specifications for either syllable.

Intonation Pattern 3, Exercise 1

Say the following words with primary stress on the first syllable and weak stress on the second syllable.

juggler	English	jewel	landing	humor	control
stumble	flashback	smaller	salesman	master	bottom
rodent	monthly	seventh	lenses	canyon	premise
imprint	offspring	license	converse	inverses	reverse
splatter	raffle	react	explore	thriving	cyclone
acid	current	actress	process	malice	chapter

PATTERN 4

—
• .

Pattern 4 is the first of the 8 patterns to be applied to three-syllable words. The first syllable is delivered with weak stress, the second syllable, primary stress, and the third syllable returns to weak stress.

Intonation Pattern 4, Exercise 1

Say the following words with weak stress on the first syllable, primary stress on the second, and weak stress on the third syllable.

ambitious	arthritis	outrageous	consistent	falsetto	isolate
Fitzgerald	approval	smokier	snappiness	umbrella	together
athletic	animal	tambourine	vacancy	dissolving	concession
Hawaii	awaken	adhesive	quadratic	iguana	acquiring
prohibit	whichever	eureka	Yolanda	simulate	resilient
measuring	treasury	composure	exposure	sulfuric	

PATTERN 5

—
• —

Intonation Pattern 5, Exercise 1

Say the following words with primary stress to the first syllable, weak stress to the second syllable, and secondary stress for the third.

civilize	amplify	burial	liberate	chloroform	cellophane
parachute	apricot	enterprise	radiant	sabotage	blasphemy
reservoir	polarize	seventy	decimal	gasoline	aliases
prosperous	humorous	octopus	delegate	compensate	centerpiece
emphasis	agitate	cultivate	misery	usefulness	sweetening
afterglow	illustrate	aftertaste	overdraft	multitude	atmosphere

PATTERN 6

—
• •

Intonation Pattern 6, Exercise 1

Say the following words with primary stress to the first syllable and weak stress for the second and third syllables.

temperature	photograph	telegraph	transference	blasphemy	pacemaker
scholarship	talkative	emphasis	prominent	attitude	acrobat
aftermath	sweetening	doctoral	octagon	benefit	novelty
alternate	intellect	fantasy	different	variant	regular
feathery	northerner	Bethany	moderate	vanity	Zachary
finally	cardinal	enterprise	tapestry	aerial	

PATTERN 7

Intonation Pattern 7, Exercise 1

Say the following words with secondary stress on the first syllable, weak stress on the second, and a falling pitch curve on the third syllable.

remember	enclosure	referee	populous	stipulate	transparent
jasper	specialize	enterprise	dominant	personnel	disconnect
southerner	westerner	furniture	external	universe	watershed
scrupulous	carrier	shortening	vertical	guarantee	introvert
introduce	attitude	furthermore	thriftily	nectarine	tangerine
manuscript	barrier	signature	casual	engineer	difference

PATTERN 8

—
— • •

The eighth and final pattern of intonation is a little more complex than the previous seven patterns, because it applies to words with four syllables.

Intonation Pattern 8, Exercise 1

Say the following words with secondary stress on the first syllable, weak stress on the second, primary stress on the third, and weak stress again on the fourth syllable.

Germination	indecision	politician	designated	disestablish
resignation	everlasting	alphabetic	isolation	fluctuation
influenza	inclination	planetary	amplifier	incoherent
Alabama	multiplier	economic	reputation	exhibition
cultivation	accidental	salutation	consequential	application
composition	unemployed	Manitoba	energetic	exclamation
publication	influential	military	preferential	Massachusetts

Special Intonation Patterns
Compound Word Patterns

The following patterns are all variations of the 8 fundamentals patterns used for **compound words** (which are made up of two words but act as a single word).

PATTERN 1

—
—

Say the following words with primary stress on the first syllable and secondary stress on the second.

Newsstand	sandbox	thumbprint	eyebrow	bedtime	handshake	aircraft
Backwash	catfish	chestnut	firework	earwax	courthouse	puffball

PATTERN 2

—
• —

Say the following words with primary stress on the first syllable, weak stress on the second, and secondary stress on the third.

rattlesnake   quarterback   copycat   scholarship   gingerbread   ladybug
crackerjack   underworld   bodywash   apple juice   butter knife scatterbrain

PATTERN 3

—
— •

Say the following words with primary stress on the first syllable, secondary stress on the second, and weak stress on the third.

blueberry   oversee   lightheaded   lawmaker   turnover   teenager
roadrunner   homecoming   windowpane   woodcutter strawberry backwater

PATTERN 4

—
• — •

Say the following words with primary stress on the first syllable, weak stress on the second, secondary stress on the third, and weak stress again on the fourth.

vice-president   poison ivy   anybody   supermarket   motorcycle   Mona Lisa
nervous system   South Pacific   Costa Rica   solar system overshadow   everybody

PATTERN 5

— • ⌒

119

Say the following words with secondary stress on the first syllable, weak stress on the second, and a fall pitch curve on the third.

oversee   copper wire   underway   aftermath   uppermost   humankind
heavyweight overtake   counterweight   buttermilk overthrow   waterfall

---

COMPOUND NOUNS

Shortstop   Railroad   Headphone   Quicksilver   Ringworm
Sandbox

Wheelchair   Searchlight   Shipwreck   Eyeball   Billboard   Armpit

ADJECTIVE AND NOUN PAIRS

Short stop   rail road   head phone   quick silver   ring worm   sand box

Wheel chair   search light   ship wreck   eye ball   billboard   armpit

NOUN-VERB HOMONYM PAIRS

The following words are **homonyms** (words that have more than one meaning but are spelled the same way). The first list of words is made up of nouns (like an "object"). Say them with primary stress on the first syllable and secondary stress on the second. The second list consists of the corresponding verbs to each noun-homonym. Say those words with weak stress on the first syllable and a falling pitch curve on the second (like when you "object" to something).

—
—

NOUNS

object extract advice affect defect contest

converse permit desert convict address subject

. ⌒

VERBS

object extract advice affect defect contest

converse permit desert convict address subject

Contrast

The differentiation of pitch and stress in syllables and the degree of that differentiation is known as **contrast**. A word with both primary stress and weak stress utilized will be high in contrast, because some part(s) is given significantly more stress.

Say the following words with the pitch and stress guides given. Listen to the contrasts between words.

Intonation at the Sentence and Phrase Level

Pitch and stress apply to the intonation of sentences as well as individual words. Mastering the use of intonation at the sentence level will allow the speaker to carry on smooth, fluent conversations. Once the speaker has become more comfortable with intonating American English at the word level, he/she can integrate those complex patterns more intuitively into sentence-level speech. This method applies a broader, more intuitive approach to sentence and phrase level conversation.

Content Words

Content words are words that fall under the categories of: nouns, verbs, adjectives and adverbs. These words hold the carry the information load of the sentence, and will be most often be the words which receive stress in sentences. There are some situations, such as sarcasm and aggression/anger, in which the articles, prepositions, or other function words (words which carry the sentence grammatically but are not in-and-of themselves informative) might be stress. However, those are very particular circumstances and are certainly not the status-quo of the American English accent.

SENTENCE	CONTENT WORDS	FUNCTION WORDS
I love you.	I, love, you	
I do not **have change** for the **bus**.	I, have, change, bus	do, not, for, the
Marten has never **seen Venice**.	Marten, seen, Venice	has, never
Where is my **ugly hat**?	Where, my, ugly, hat	is
Theresa is in **town**.	Theresa, town	is, in
The **printer** is **out** of **toner**.	printer, out, toner	The, is, of
Run over **here**.	Run, here	over
Do the **dishes**, please!	Do, dishes	the, please
I need to **talk** to **you** about **yesterday**.	I, need, talk, you, yesterday	to, to, about

SENTENCE	CONTENT WORDS	FUNCTION WORDS
Where is **Seamus**?	Where, Seamus	is
Your boot smells awful.	Your, boot, smells, awful	
Adam is **pleasant** this **evening.**	Adam, pleasant, evening	is, this
Where is **all** of the **mayonnaise**?	Where, all, mayonnaise	is, of, the

Focal Words in Intonation

Say the following sentence with no particular inflections.

    I enjoyed the show.

Now try saying the same sentence with primary stress on the first word. This indicates that the word is the highlight of the sentence.

    I enjoyed the show.

A focal word is similar to the subject, but a focal word does not necessarily have to be a noun. If the most significant idea in a sentence is the verb, then it is the focal word.

    I **enjoyed** the show.

Now the focal word is "enjoyed" and not "I". The speaker's primary emphasis is that the show was enjoyable, not that he/she was the person who enjoyed it.

Say the following sentences with no particular inflection the first time, then with primary stress on the first word (to show that the subject of the sentence is the focal tone), and finally with primary stress on the verb (to show that the verb is the highlight).

She believes that man.
She believes that man.
She **believes** that man.

We went to the theatre.
We went to the theatre.
We **went** to the theatre.

I passed my final exam.
I passed my final exam.
I **passed** my final exam.

You should wash your hands.
You should wash your hands.
You should **wash** your hands.

He won first prize.
He won first prize.
He **won** first prize.

Questions

Interrogative sentences (those which ask a question) can be broken into two categories, those which utilize the questions words (where, when, what, which, who, whom, why, and how) and those which make a requests, ask yes/no questions, or express skepticism (i.e. "Tom said that?").

Say the following questions with a falling pitch curve on the last word.

Where did you go?
Why did you bring this?
How is it?
What is your point?
When are we leaving?
Which one did you like?
What are you looking for?
Where is my dog?
Why is the floor sticky?
How much does this cost?
When is the party?
Which way did they go?

Say the following requests with a rising pitch curve on the last word.

> May I have tea? (request)
> Can you handle that? (skepticism)
> Should I bring my sleeping bag? (yes/no)
> You think he's ready? (skepticism)
> Would you like to dance? (request)
> Did you enjoy the opera? (yes/no)

Statement vs. Question

Say the following sentences with a falling pitch curve on the last word to show that it is a statement, something the speaker knows. Then, say it again with a rising pitch curve to show that it is a question, something the speaker does not know, does not understand, or is not convinced of.

I'm lucky.
I'm lucky?

Jackie is a good student.
Jackie is a good student?

Juan went fishing.
Juan when fishing?

Pluto is no longer a planet.
Pluto is no longer a planet?

There are multiple ways to give inflection to any statement. One could say "Jackie is a good student" with no particular inflection, which would sound dispassionate and robotic.

Jackie is a good student – implies that there are good students, and it is most important that Jackie is one of them.

Jackie is a **good** student – implies that Jackie is a student, but it is most important that she is a good one.

Jackie is a good student? – implies skepticism or a lack of understanding of how/why she is a good student.

Jackie is a **good** student? – implies that while it is known Jackie is a student, it was not previously understood that she is a good student.

Jackie is a good student? – implies that of all good students, the speaker did not know that Jackie was one of them.

You're the last in line – implies that you are in fact the last person in the line.

You're the **last** in line– implies that you are in line, but more importantly the last person in the line.

You're the **last** in line? – implies that while there is a line, you are the last in line.

You're the last in line? – implies skepticism or a lack of understanding of how/why you are the last person in the line.

You're the first in line? – implies that the speaker was expecting someone to be the last in line, but not necessarily you.

I won – implies that while someone has one, most importantly that someone was the speaker ("I")

I **won** – implies that the speaker has done something important, the speaker has won.

I won?– implies that the speaker is

I **won**?–

This sofa only costs a hundred dollars– implies skepticism or a lack of understanding of how/why the sofa costs only a hundred dollars.

This sofa only costs a hundred dollars– implies that that out of all the sofas, this sofa is a good bargain at only a hundred dollars.

This sofa **only** costs a hundred dollars– implies that the sofa is not a bargain at only a hundred dollars.

This sofa only costs a **hundred** dollars? – implies skepticism or a lack of understanding of how/why the sofa costs only a hundred dollars. The price of the sofa is the new/surprising information that the speaker is responding to.

Complex and Compound Sentences

Some messages contain multiple subjects, focal words, and/or can be longer, thusly adding to the rhythm of the message. Other sentences contain two complete clauses (a clause is an idea with a complete subject and a complete predicate) combined into one sentence with a conjunction. These sentences can be complementary to one another (often using the conjunction *and*) or may show some sort of contrast (often using *but* or *however*). Say the following pairs of sentences, paying particular attention to the bolded/stressed words. Then try to identify which of the words in the sentence are content words and which are function words. Keep in mind that a conjunction can be a content word, especially if it emphasizes the two sentences or phrases as complementary or contrasting.

I called Joe **all night**, but I **couldn't** reach him.

SENTENCE   CONTENT WORDS   FUNCTION WORDS

I **called** Joe all night, **but** I couldn't reach him.

SENTENCE   CONTENT WORDS   FUNCTION WORDS

They will either go **home**, or they will watch a **movie**.

SENTENCE   CONTENT WORDS   FUNCTION WORDS

They will **either** go home, **or** they will watch a movie.

SENTENCE   **CONTENT WORDS**   **FUNCTION WORDS**

I **like** my car, and I got it for a **good** price.

SENTENCE   **CONTENT WORDS**   **FUNCTION WORDS**

I **like** my car, **and** I got it for a good price.

SENTENCE   **CONTENT WORDS**   **FUNCTION WORDS**

Lisa **is** a smart worker; however, she does **not** get along with others.

SENTENCE   **CONTENT WORDS**   **FUNCTION WORDS**

Lisa is a smart worker; **however**, she does **not** get along with others.

SENTENCE   **CONTENT WORDS**   **FUNCTION WORDS**

Linking

Words have a tendency to run together when spoken in phrases and sentences. Though the meaning of the sentence is made up of separate words, the vocalization of those words is broken into sound groups. Those sound groups are not isolated within each word, rather they overlap, and the last syllable of one word may appear in a sound grouping before the beginning of a new word. Particular sounds at the end of a word can also affect the pronunciation of the sound at the beginning of the next word. Sometimes this effect is simply a matter of adjusting vowel length or sound grouping, and other times two sounds combine into a single sound that is different from both previous sounds.

When he /t/ sound at the end of a word is followed by a /y/ (at the beginning of the next word) in a question (often involving a contraction followed by the word you), there is a blending of the /t/ and /y/ sounds into a single /tʃ/ sound that bridges two words. This blending is especially common in colloquial speech. It is not unacceptable in more formal speak, though it does not necessarily sound unnatural to simply pronounce the /t/ and the /y/ separately.

Don't you think so?

Now try integrating the /tʃ/

Don-choo think so?

Wouldn't you like to go home?

Wouldn-choo like to go home?

When /d/ is the final phoneme of a word and /y/ is the initial phoneme of the next word (again, usually in the form of the word you), the sounds then combine similarly to the previous example. The difference is that /d/ and /y/ produce a /dʒ/ instead of a /tʃ/.

You want me to lend you a dollar?

Now try integrating the /dʒ/

You want me to len-joo a dollar?

Could you go home first?

Cou-joo go home first?

If a word in a phrase ends with a consonant and the next word begins with a vowel, group that consonant sound with the vowel sound. The consonant sound is attached to the first syllable of the next word.

Notice the flow of the 2 syllables in the word "picket" (pi-ket)

If instead of saying "picket", one were to say "pick at it", the syllable grouping would be very similar: pi-kat-it.

The same would be true if one were to say "pick it out": pi-kit-out.

Examples:

John is a nice boy.

Jo-ni-sa-nice-boy.

Give us

Gi-vus

fasten it

fa-su-nit

tap her arm

ta-per-arm

given ⌢his particular tastes

giv-enis-par-ti-cular-tastes

It works ⌢if you try.

It-work-sif-you-try.

Does that girl ⌢ever slow down?

Does-that-gir-lever-slow-down?

When the final sound of a word in a sentence or phrase is a plosive consonant (/p/, /b/, /k/, /g/, /t/, /d/), that sound is said at almost the same time as the first consonant sound in the following word. This linking scenario is only true if the second word begins with a consonant, since words beginning with vowels would follow the examples in the previous list.

Examples:

keep ⌢driving

bathtub ⌢time

take ⌢that

leg ⌢support

sit ⌢down

good ⌢boy

Links between words where the first word ends in a consonant and the second word begins with the same consonant, that sound is held to last both words instead of being pronounced twice.

Examples:

Will likes you.

big guy

Sam made it.

last time

Those jewels shine nicely on you.

with this salad

Emphasis of Word Segments

In some situations, speakers will need to place stress on segments of a word, but not the entire word. This usually occurs when it is necessary to express the difference between two words. Read the following sentences aloud and only place emphasis on the fragments of words that are stressed. Notice that this need for clarification often occurs in the prefixes or suffixes of words.

Did you say you would dissect him?

No, I said that I would di**rect** him.

My intention was to **de**construct his theory.

Despite his wit, the boy seemed **un**educated.

She is not being super**vised**; she is the super**visor**.

Segmented emphasis is also frequently used in poetry and lyrical speak. Properly used, it aligns words that rhyme, have similar rhythms, or are alliterations (groups of words that begin with the same sound).

But off in the **dis**tance stood
a man in need of my as**sis**tance
a man eight feet **height**ened
named Nate, tall and **bright**ened by the sun
The **p**owerful **p**rince's heart **p**alpitated with **p**assion.

Sir, you aren't **listen**ing to me. You have to move your car.
We are go**ing** to the store, so we are not there yet.

Rudeness

With non-native speakers, the ability to sound rude comes more naturally than the speech itself. What sounds polite to communicator's ear may sound rude, abrasive, or sarcastic to a native-speaker's ear. Placing stress on the wrong word or syllable will make your speech sound angry or hostile, even misplaced pitch curves can get a non-native speaker into trouble.

Example:

Marci, where did you go?

Marci, where did you **go**? – implies that the speaker is upset at Marci for not clarifying where she was going, and is upset at where she might have been.

Marci, where did you go? – implies that the speaker merely wishes to find out where Marci had been, notice the lack of hostility. This is because a falling pitch curve, as is customary for questions, is used on the last word in the sentence.

In the example above the stress was placed on the verb. In cases of unnecessary verb stress, the native-speaker's ear finds this speech full of accusation.

What do the misplaced stresses and/or pitch curves accuse or imply in the following sentences?

What are you **doing**?
How much did you **say** you make per hour?
Sally was just **sitting** there.
Why would you **say** that?
I am **reading**.
Do you **understand**?
I **feel** sick.
You did not **call** me last night.
I **know** what I am **doing**.
Why don't you **stop** and **ask** for directions?

Now that the misplaces stresses and/or pitch curves have been explained, place the appropriate marks for stress and pitch down below, then explain what idea the speaker is trying to convey.

What are you doing?
How much did you say you make per hour?
Sally was just sitting there.
Why would you say that?
I am reading.
Do you understand?
I feel sick.
You did not call me last night.
I know what I am doing.
Why don't you stop and ask for directions?

Conversation Exercises

Read aloud to yourself, a speech pathologist, or with a peer to identify the context of the dialogue. **Describe what stresses and intonations tell you about the speakers.**

Exercise One:

Mike and Ana are purchasing tickets from the local Cineplex for a matinee showing of the newest summer blockbuster.

Mike: I heard this movie received three stars.
Ana: Meagan said she didn't like it, though.
Mike: Meagan doesn't know what she's talking about.
Clerk: How many tickets, sir?
Mike: Two tickets for the 6 o'clock showing please.
Clerk: I am afraid the 6 o'clock showing is sold out.
Ana: Good. I didn't want to see it anyway.
Clerk: Perhaps another show?
Mike: Sure that would be great.

Now, on a blank sheet of paper write the dialogue down. Then change the stress words and intonations to give the dialogue a whole new meaning.

Exercise Two:

Ben and Matt are discussing their grades at the end of a college semester.
Ben: Hey, Matt, how did you do in Professor Robertson's physics class?
Matt: I haven't checked yet.
Ben: Why not?
Matt: Because I'm afraid that I may have failed.
Ben: I'm sure you did fine! You're such a good student, you know.
Matt: You think so?

Now, on a blank sheet of paper write the dialogue down. Then change the stress words and intonations to give the dialogue a whole new meaning.

Exercise Three:

Alan is trying to ask Kathy out on a date.
Alan: Kathy.
Kathy: Yes?
Alan: Would you like to go out sometime? You know, have a coffee?
Kathy: I'd love to Alan.

Now, on a blank sheet of paper write the dialogue down. Then change the stress words and intonations to give the dialogue a whole new meaning.

Exercise Four:

A police officer has just pulled over Marcus for speeding.
Marcus: Is there a problem, Officer?
Officer: License and registration, please.
Marcus: Here you are.
Officer: Do you know how fast you were going?
Marcus: I don't know, officer.
Officer: I clocked you at a hundred and twelve.
Marcus: I'm sure I wasn't going that fast.
Officer: Step out of the vehicle, sir.
Marcus: What?
Officer: Step out of the vehicle sir.

Now, on a blank sheet of paper write the dialogue down. Then change

the stress words and intonations to give the dialogue a whole new meaning.

Exercise Five:

Rachael and Tom are co-workers at a small furniture store.
Rachael: Did you check the bolts on the console table?
Tom: No, but I'll take care of it.
Rachael: What are you doing at the moment?
Tom: Counting the money in my cash register.
Rachael: But you aren't closing for another hour.
Tom: I know, I just prefer to count the money regularly to make sure it's all there. Do you dislike the idea?
Rachael: No. In fact, I think it's very responsible.

Exercise Six:

Grandpa asks his grandson what he would spend money on.
Grandpa: Anthony, what would you do if I gave you a dollar?
Anthony: I would by an ice cream, Grandpa.
Grandpa: And if I gave you two dollars?
Anthony: I'd buy one for me and one for you.
Grandpa: And if I gave you a third dollar?
Anthony: I'd save it.
Grandpa: Why not save the other two dollars?
Anthony: Because I'd like an ice cream now and mama always said to share, so I'd have to get you one. But if I save the last dollar I can have an ice cream all to myself tomorrow.

Exercise Eight:

Pablo and Francisco are cousins, meeting for the first time in ten years.
Pablo: Francisco. Good to see you. How have you been?
Francisco: Fine, just fine. And you?
Pablo: Couldn't be better. What have you been doing lately?
Francisco: I finally received my degree after three years.
Pablo: What degree did you receive?
Francisco: A Masters in Dance.

Exercise Nine:

Hector is proposing to Athena.

Hector: Athena, will you marry me?
Athena: I will have to think about it.
Hector: What is there to think about?
Athena: How much did you say your bonus was?

Exercise Ten:

Mr. Mann is terminating Nathan's employment and cutting his benefits.

Mr. Mann: Nathan. Good job on the Anderson Case.
Nathan: Thank you, sir.
Mr. Mann: Although it pains me to say, the Anderson Case fell through and the CEOs want to do a few cut backs.
Nathan: What do you mean?
Mr. Mann: I don't know how I can be any clearer. You can use your lunch hour to clean out your desk and vacate the premises
Nathan: But, sir! I have been employed here for over twenty years. I can't retire now.
Mr. Mann: No I don't imagine that you will. Your pension plan has expired, and I'm afraid that appeals to reapply can only be done by active employees.
Nathan: I can't believe this.
Mr. Mann: Well, it was a pleasure working with you, Nathan. You're a real go-getter. You'll be fine.
Nathan: Can I at least use you as a reference.
Mr. Mann: I don't think I would be comfortable with you doing that.

BIBLIOGRAPHY

American Speech-Language-Hearing Association (2011). The clinical education of students with accents. Accessed 1 June 2012 from http://www.asha.org/docs/html/PI2011-00324.html.

Bruijnzeels, M. & Visser, A. (2005). Intercultural doctor-patient relational outcomes: need more to be studied, Patient Education and Counseling, 57(2), 151-152.

Bent, T., & Bradlow, A. R. (2003). The interlanguage speech intelligibility benefit. *The Journal of the Acoustical Society of America, 114,* 1600–1610.

Bradlow, A. R., Akahane-Yamada, R., Pisoni, D. B., & Tohkura, Y. (1999). Training Japanese listeners to identify English /r/ and /l/: Long-term retention of learning in perception and production. *Perception & Psychophysics, 61,* 977–985.

Bradlow, A. R., & Bent, T. (2008). Perceptual adaptation to non-native speech. *Cognition, 106,* 707–729.

Brady, K. W., Duewer, N., & King, A. M. (2016). The effectiveness of a multimodal vowel-targeted intervention in accent modification.*Contemporary Issues in Communication Science and Disorders, 43,* 23–34.

Carlson, H. K., & McHenry, M. A. (2006). Effect of accent and dialect on employability. *Journal of Employment Counseling, 43* (2), 70–83.

Celce-Murcia, M., Brinton, D. M., & Goodwin, J. M. (1996). *Teaching pronunciation: A reference for teachers of English to speakers of other languages.* Cambridge, United Kingdom: Cambridge University Press.

Chen, P.G., Curry, L.A., Bernheim, S.M., Berg, D., Nunez-Smith, M. & Gozu, A. (2011). Professional challenges of non-U.S.-born international medical graduates and recommendations for support during residency training, Academic Medicine, 86(11), 1383-1388.

Christensen, Barbara (September 13, 2017). "What is Accent Resuction." *Accent Freedom*. Retrieved 11 January 2018.

Dorgan K.A., Lange, F., Floyd, M. & Kemp, E. (2009). International medical graduate—patient communication: a qualitative analysis of perceived barriers, Academic Medicine, 84(11), 1567- 1575.

Eggly, S., Musial, J., & Smulowitz, J. (1999). The relationship between English language proficiency and success as a medical resident, English for Specific Purposes, 18(2), 201-208. Friedman, M., Sutnick, A.I., Stillman, P.L., Norcini, J.J. et al. (1991). The use of standardized patients to evaluate the spoken-English proficiency of foreign medical graduates, Academic Medicine, 66(9), 61-63.

Friedman, M., Sutnick, A.I., Stillman, P.L., Regan, M.B. & Norcini, J.J. (1993). The relationship of spoken-English proficiencies of foreign medical school graduates to their clinical competence, Academic Medicine, 68(10), pp1-3.

Hahn, L. (2004). Primary stress and intelligibility: Research to motivate the teaching of suprasegmentals. *TESOL Quarterly, 38*, 201–223.

Hope, Donna (2006). *American English Pronunciation: It's No Good Unless You're Understood*. Cold Wind Press. p. 10. ISBN 1-58631-050-X

Kelly, P. (2013) Discussions re. Communication Skills and Speech Training with Katrina Dahl, 2012-2013

Kramer, M. (2006). Educational challeges of international medical graduates in psychiatric residencies, Journal of the American Academy of Psychoanalysis and Dynamic Psychiatry, 34(1), 163-171.
Kurtz, S., Silverman, J. & Draper, J. (2004). Teaching and learning communication skills in medicine, Radcliffe Publishing Ltd., Oxford.

Levy, E. S., & Law, F. F. (2010). Production of French vowels by American-English learners of French: Language experience, consonantal context, and the perception-production relationship. *The Journal of the Acoustical Society of America, 128,* 1290–1305.

Luongo, M.T. (2004). Accent reduction as sound investment, International Herald Tribune. Accessed 1 June 2012 from http://www.highbeam.com/doc/1P1-140232319.html#

Morley, J. (1996). Second language speech/pronunciation: Acquisition, instructions, standards, variation, and accent. In J. E. Alatis, C. A. Straelhle, M. Ronkin, & B. Gallenberger (Eds.), *Current trends and future prospects* (pp. 140–160). Washington, DC: Georgetown University Press.

Moyer, A. (1999). Ultimate attainment in L2 phonology. *Studies in Second Language Acquisition, 21*, 81–108.

Munro, M. J., & Derwing, T. M. (1995). Foreign accent, comprehensibility, and intelligibility in the speech of second language learners. *Language Learning, 45*, 73–97.

Ruane, L. (2010). Professors of pronunciation help immigrants, USA Today. Accessed 26 March 2012 from http://www.usatoday.com/news/nation/2010-09-10-accentclasses10_ST_N.html

Schevitz, T. (1999). Instructors' accents make lessons hard, students say, San Francisco Chronicle. Accessed 20 May 2012 from http://www.sfgate.com/cgi-bin/article.cgi?f=/c/a/1999/11/27/MN23448.DTL#ixzz1qFTPWI8s

Schmidt, A. M. (1997). Working with adult foreign accent: Strategies for intervention.*Contemporary Issues in Communication Science and Disorders , 24*,53–62.
Sikorski, L. D. (2005). Regional accents: A rationale for intervening and competencies required. *Seminars in Speech and Language, 26*(2), 118–125.

Thompson, M.J., Hagopian, A., Fordyce, M. & Hart, L.G. (2009). Do international medical graduates (IMGs) "fill the gap" in rural primary care in the United States? A national study, Journal of Rural Health, 25(2), 124-134.

Ulrey, K.L. & Amason, P. (2001). Intercultural communication between patients and health care providers: an exploration of intercultural communication effectiveness cultural sensitivity, stress, and anxiety, Health Communication, 13(4), 449-463.

www.ingramcontent.com/pod-product-compliance
Lightning Source LLC
LaVergne TN
LVHW061311060426
835507LV00019B/2107